STOCKS BONDS & MUTUAL FUNDS

STOCKS BONDS & MUTUAL FUNDS

Joseph Newman — Directing Editor

U.S. NEWS & WORLD REPORT BOOKS

A division of U.S.News & World Report, Inc.

WASHINGTON, D.C.

Contents

Illustrations

Acknowledgments

In preparing this book, the editors of *U.S.News & World Report Books* have had the assistance of a number of specialists. They are indebted above all to Sidney Margolius, a prominent specialist in family financial affairs, for his major contribution to the manuscript, and to Robert Amon, a researcher and writer on economic affairs. For their research and guidance, a word of appreciation is also due to Gerald Lenaghan; Samuel Braude, an over-the-counter specialist; Norman Freed, arbitrage and investment specialist; and Harold S. Oberg, investment company research. Fred Cohn, of Johnson's Charts, and John Adams, of the Investment Company Institute, helped in the preparation of charts and tables. Harold Taylor worked with Linda Glisson and Roslyn Grant, of the book division, in editing the final version of the manuscript and keeping it up-to-date.

The flag-bedecked entrance to the New York Stock Exchange as seen from the steps of the U.S. Treasury Building.

CHAPTER 1

What
This
Book Is
About

This book is designed for middle-income investors. It has been planned and written as an objective guide. Its underlying premise is that the practical investor seeks not only to increase his capital but also to preserve it.

Unlike books of the "Anyone Can Make A Million" type, this guide aims to help the investor of moderate income develop a sophisticated personal investment program, integrated into his way of life.

Protecting and managing one's money effectively deserves at least the kind of attention a prudent man gives to such protective routines as visiting the doctor and dentist, servicing the automobile, and maintaining the family home. Such attention is essential, if the money one saves is not to be eaten away by inflation.

What is the likelihood that the continuous decline in the purchasing power of the dollar will be checked? It has never happened, historians tell us, neither in the 200-year history of the United States nor in any other country, as far back as the earliest civilizations. Sometimes slow, sometimes fast, currency depreciation is an endless process. And if we don't care for history, we can see what happens from day to day at the supermarket check-out counter.

In most cases, therefore, the middle-income earner no longer asks, "Should I invest?" Instead he wants to know, "In what should I invest?"

The ideal investment, which unfortunately does not exist, would have four characteristics:

1. It would be completely safe from loss.

2. It would be liquid or readily convertible into cash.

3. It would return a high rate of interest or dividend.

4. It would grow in value as fast as the increase in the cost of living, or faster.

The problem of the investor, now as always, is to find the combination of these attributes that best suits his circumstances. Today, the fourth objective—some hedge against inflation—is foremost in most investors' minds. Primarily to achieve that goal, about 32 million Americans now have an investment stake in stocks through direct ownership, and millions more are involved indirectly through mutual funds, pension funds, or other pooled forms of investment.

Inducements to invest are greater today than ever before. Conservative brokers who once advised "soundness and seasoning" for small investors are now recommending investments in new growth industries. Mutual fund shares are offered not only by traditional investment dealers but also by insurance salesmen, finance companies, tax services, and even department stores. Such speculative investments as participations in oil drilling ventures, once reserved for wealthy adventurers, now attract middle-income investors.

There are dangers in the spread of familiarity with stock market dealing, however. Some securities salesmen, who are concerned with their own commissions, encourage their customers to buy and sell stocks without realistically appraising their value or considering the safety of long-term investments.

In recent years investors seeking quick capital gains have been enticed by temporary sharp advances in overpriced new stock issues. They have bought into purported growth companies, inadequately financed conglomerates, and fads such as bowling alleys, franchised chains, nursing homes, and computer software. Many investors have been badly burned.

Investors may also be misled by accounting practices that inflate apparent earnings, by the recommendations of brokers more concerned with their commissions than with their clients, and by the initial successes of daring fund managers. Brokerage houses themselves are not immune to financial disaster; a failure can leave the investor with his funds locked up and no way to rearrange his holdings in a falling market.

Even investors in sound situations may become discouraged by the sharp drops in the market which have become inevitable as institutions dominate trading. When all those big bodies head for the door at the same time, someone will get trampled.

The investor must guard against the attitude of Mark Twain's cat, which having once burnt itself on a hot stove lid thereafter refused to curl up on a warm one. Similarly, the investor may miss the chance to recoup when an upturn comes.

The 1975 stock market turnaround which began recovery from the minidepression of 1974 offered excellent investment opportunities. Investing at that point, however, required not only courage and foresight but also the wisdom to have taken one's losses in 1973-74 and saved cash for an upturn.

Continued recovery in 1976 brought new problems. A bright spot in 1974-75 had been the emergence of high-interest short-term paper which offered a haven in the economic storm. As recovery progressed, however, banks were filled with money before capital investment strengthened to absorb the funds. Thus interest rates declined. Housing starts, on the other hand, recovered earlier than usual, thereby allowing savings institutions to offer good rates for medium-term investments.

Alertness to changing market phases requires more effort than just buying a bond or a solid stock that one can "put away and forget." But the extra attention pays off. This is true for the small investor as well as the large. In some ways the small investor is at a disadvantage, but there are ways to mitigate this handicap. This book is designed to point out those ways.

The small investor has two major problems. One is the relative difficulty of diversifying small investments. The other is the task of securing accurate and timely information. The large investor can engage a professional adviser whose business is to ferret out all the information available, get it early, and analyze it thoroughly. However, there are ways for the small investor to do this job himself if he is willing to work at it.

One need not be rich to develop an investment program. The median household income of all shareholders was estimated in 1975 at about $17,000. The largest investor groups are not wealthy businessmen or professional people, but housewives and retirees. You do not need a huge sum of disposable money for sound, sophisticated investing, but you do need a definite program.

1. *Key your investment policy to your investment potential and your needs and goals.*

The first step is to make a realistic appraisal of the time you can devote to investing and the money you can invest. Each method of investment has its advantages; in different situations, at different times of life, each has its special appeal.

A young family usually seeks growth. Earning power is expected to rise. Higher income now can be traded for capital gains later. The older person, especially if he is retired, cannot wait for growth. He needs maximum income and minimum risk. Logically, these differing needs dictate what portion of savings should go into stocks and mutual funds or into bonds and mortgage trusts.

Tax-exempt bonds and other tax-sheltered investments may be important during middle age; earnings are at their peak, dependents have left home, and the interest-deductible mortgage has been paid off. Tax exemption is of little interest to the young family and of less to the retired man or nonworking widow.

2. *Remain alert and open to change.*

No one type of investment can claim all virtues at all times. Many factors affect the desirability of investment media. Many an investor tends to narrow his interest to stock in general or one category of stock, such as utilities. In a time of double-digit inflation, with rates always lagging behind costs, the utility follower cannot win, even if his command of formal security analysis is perfect. He must move to something that suits the times.

One important trend of which the small investor is learning to take advantage has the formidable name of "disintermediation." This means simply that the investor bypasses the banks and insurance companies—the conventional intermediaries—and invests directly in the instruments the intermediaries themselves favor. In this way he gains the fee the banks or insurance companies charge, as they must, for their services.

One difficulty, until recently, has been that the high-yielding short-term money market has catered to big lenders. A big bank's certificate of deposit could rarely be found in a lower denomination than $100,000. Now there are funds which buy these large CDs, and the short-term paper of commercial houses, and sell participations at retail. The Dreyfus Corporation has a large one. Brokers are happy to help customers keep the proceeds of a stock sale in such a fund, rather than see the money disappear into a security of longer maturity which will not yield another commission.

3. *Balance investments.*

Stocks, as we shall see, fall naturally into categories. We shall examine income issues, growth stocks, defensive stocks, businessmen's risks, and speculations. As we mentioned earlier, a young family probably will be interested in growth and an older one in income. However, a prudent investor will have a mixture of both.

Similarly, while concentrating funds in a few stocks offers the greatest chance for capital gain, the small investor can gain the advantages of diversification by investing in a mutual fund as well. If something goes wrong with one or two stock issues, he has some measure of protection.

For maximum safety and income, the proportion of stocks and fixed-interest securities should be varied as changing stock prices and shifting interest rates suggest. One might start, say, with $15,000 to invest, half in stocks and mutual funds, half in high-yielding bonds and mortgage-trust participations. When stock prices seem too high, funds should be shifted toward bonds. When bond prices rise to where their yield is unattractive, it is time to buy stocks. That is what conservative professional money managers do; they switch back and forth between stocks and bonds at what they judge to be the right times in the recurring cycles of stock prices vs. bond yields.

Short-term and long-term investments should also be segregated. Funds that may be needed in three or four years should go into securities with short maturities so the money will be there when it is needed. In general, only long-range savings should go into long-term investments, the values of which may fluctuate widely in the interim.

The table on page 21 shows the comparative percentage yields of various types of savings and investments. The figure of 9 percent a year for stocks includes dividends and capital gains; it is the average combined return over the last decade. For example, a family might set a feasible goal of doubling its investment capital in ten years. This would call for a combination of investments yielding 7 percent a year. With this in mind, $18,000 of investment funds might be distributed as follows:

$5,000 in savings bonds and passbooks at 5½%	$275
$8,000 in preferred stocks at 8%	640
$5,000 in corporate bonds at 9%	450
	$1,365

In addition to the 7 percent yield, this combination allows a little for the tax liabilities of the current-account part of the yield.

There is nothing magic about doubling capital in ten years. Depending on his income stability, his family needs, and his propensity to venture or to play it safe, the investor might aim at faster gains with stocks or slower but more assured increases with fixed-income securities.

4. *Select; don't wait to be sold.*

As we have noted, these are times of intense sales pressure for different types of investment. Salesmen, naturally, speak up for their own wares. Your job is to select, first, from among the various types of investment, and then from among the specific companies offering that type. For example, when you examine mutual funds, you will find an array of investment goals, a wide range of performances, and a scale of commissions ranging from nothing to more than 8 percent of your investment.

What Your Capital Can Earn*

Percentage Yields of Different Investments

Savings accounts	5-5½ %
Long-term savings certificates	6½-8¼
Growth-type mutual funds	1-3
Income-type mutual funds	5-7
Money market funds	7-8
Closed-end investment companies	5-7
Common stocks—general	5½
Growth stocks	1-3
Income stocks	7-9
Insurance stocks	3-5
Bank stocks	5-7
Preferred stocks	8-9
Corporate bonds	8-9
Tax-exempt municipal bonds	6
Ninety-day Treasury bills	5
U.S. Government bonds	5½
Mortgages	8½-9

* Typical earnings as of 1976. Does not include capital gains or losses. Long-term combined dividend and capital-gain return from stocks is approximately 9 percent a year.

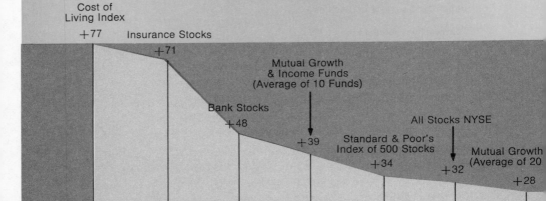

Cost of
Living Index
+77   Insurance Stocks
                +71

                        Mutual Growth
                        & Income Funds
                        (Average of 10 Funds)

          Bank Stocks   All Stocks NYSE
            +48   Mutual Growth
                              +39   Standard & Poor's   (Average of 20
                                     Index of 500 Stocks   +32
                                              +34   +28

Source: Johnson's Charts

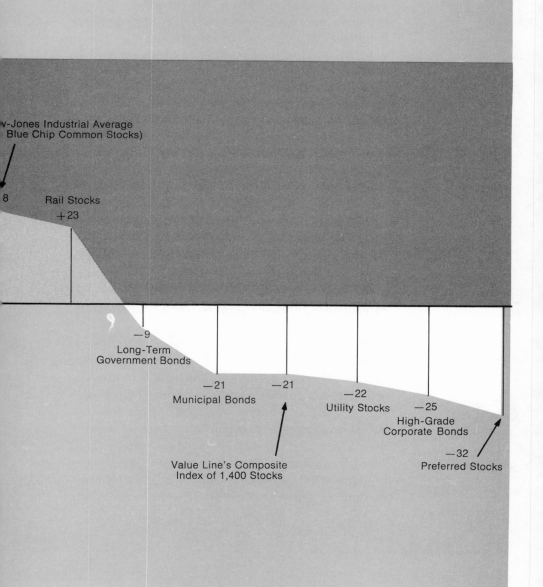

How the Value of Capital Can Change

**Prices of Stocks and Bonds Compared With Increased Cost of Living
Over 10-Year Period, 1967 to end-1976**

v-Jones Industrial Average
Blue Chip Common Stocks)

8

Rail Stocks
+23

−9
Long-Term
Government Bonds

−21
Municipal Bonds

−21

−22
Utility Stocks

−25
High-Grade
Corporate Bonds

−32
Preferred Stocks

Value Line's Composite
Index of 1,400 Stocks

Selection also involves being your own police-
man to some extent. Government regulation stops
short of guaranteeing the safety of an investment,
and even the government regulation that exists is
sometimes evaded. Even the most scrupulous
salesmen may be carried away by the temporary
popularity of some type of investment.

Sharp accounting practices may overstate the
likelihood that reported earnings will become actual cash in the till. Many investors were lured
into the recent boom-and-bust in certain franchise
stocks by such practices. The companies had included the face values of sales contracts as earnings, no matter how little of the face value had
been received as a down payment.

As with any other purchase, it is never wise to
rely totally on the verbal assurances of investment
salesmen. What counts is what is written into the
sales contract of a mutual fund or the prospectus
of a new stock issue. Prospectuses are not easy to
read, and investors often fail to study the fine
print before committing their funds. The corporate report, another useful source of information,
is covered in Chapter 7.

Sometimes an investor who has little time to
monitor his investments will open a discretionary
account, thereby permitting the broker to buy and
sell without advance authorization. Selecting a
broker for this role requires careful consideration.
Stock brokerage is a commission business; salesmen are under pressure to produce orders. Thus
there is a temptation to "churn" a discretionary
account—that is, to buy and sell stocks for an
account in order to earn additional commissions.

5. *Minimize taxes on investment earnings.*

Tax shelter is as important to the investor of moderate income as it is to those who are wealthy. With tax-sheltered investments money grows faster in the sense that more of it goes to work earlier. It does not take a very large income to incur a 30 percent tax these days. Consequently a sheltered 7 percent return is equal to a taxed 10 percent.

Methods used by large investors to hold down their tax liabilities are detailed in Chapter 18; these are available to the smaller investor as well. As yields from tax-exempt "municipals"—obligations of states, cities, and taxing districts—mentioned in Chapter 12 have increased, they have been issued in smaller denominations to interest moderate investors.

6. *Invest time as well as money.*

Often a husband and wife who have accumulated $10,000 or $15,000 in years of working and saving will decide that it is time to invest in stocks. They make a list and commit the entire sum in one order, giving the transaction less thought than they would devote to buying a $300 refrigerator.

Conventional wisdom two generations ago was that it was possible to identify an industry leader, buy its shares, and "lock them up and forget them." That is the road to disaster in this mature economy of 213 million people. Stocks need constant reevaluation. Profitability varies from industry to industry as conditions change. Companies rise and fall. Market fashions provide opportunities for switching.

7. *Everyone needs a nest egg.*

Some part of everyone's savings should be kept

How $10,000 Can Grow

Record of Different Investments
Over 10-Year Period

	Original Investment (Jan. 1, 1967)	After 10 Years (Jan. 1, 1977)
All mutual funds average*	$10,000	$17,181
5% interest, compounded quarterly	10,000	16,436
Savings and loan associations**	10,000	16,309
Commercial banks time and savings deposits**	10,000	16,024
Government savings bonds (Series E)	10,000	15,050
Growth mutual funds average*	10,000	14,669
Corporate (Aaa) bonds***	10,000	13,933
Standard & Poor's 500 Stock Index****	10,000	13,377

* Assumes reinvestment of all dividends and capital gains distributions.

** Original investment compounded annually by average annual yields.

*** Interest reinvested; bond prices reduced to market value.

**** All dividends reinvested.

Sources: Lipper Analytical Services, United States League of Savings Associations

Ten Tested Principles For Practical Investors

1. Never put all your eggs in one basket; diversify both horizontally (different stocks) and vertically (different types of investments).

2. Be alert to changes in different types of investments in relation to each other, such as the prevailing interest rates on bonds and mortgages versus stocks.

3. Read the business news carefully; watch out for new buying trends, important new products, and new industry and consumer needs.

4. Watch social changes and trends in public interests—from what people wear to what they drive; from how they spend vacations to how they feed their families.

5. Aim to buy when values are good and to sell when price-earnings ratios become exaggerated. But never expect to buy at the actual bottom or to sell at the actual top of the market.

6. Review your investments whenever there is a change such as a general price movement or a change in the earnings patterns, prospects, or market prices of the stocks you own.

7. Don't let yourself be "sold" on an investment; "shop" for the best values in competing investments—different mutual funds, various stocks that meet your investment objectives.

8. Know your own investment abilities and objectives; what may be a suitable approach for someone else may not fit your circumstances.

9. Know the tax rules in order to maximize your investment earnings by taking advantage of all possible "shelter."

10. Wait for a buying opportunity instead of plunging in when market prices are high and speculative fever is at a peak.

in fixed-value form such as E bonds or passbook savings accounts. Funds that will be needed to meet basic family needs should never go into common stocks or mutual funds. Whatever a salesman may tell you, such shares are not a dependable way in which to save for such costs as school expenses for older children. A youngster cannot wait for college tuition while stocks or fund shares recover from their periodic and inevitable dips in value.

The conventional wisdom is that the E bond and the passbook account do not keep pace with inflation and that the only way to hedge against rising costs is to buy stocks. This is only partly true. Although in the long run stocks may keep pace with the rise in prices, or even do better, they do not always rise at the same time as living costs. For example, in 1973-74 inflation rose to a frightening degree while stocks suffered losses comparable in some instances to those of the Great Depression.

2

Building
Your
Own
Portfolio

The question today in most households able to invest is not whether to own stocks, but rather how to go about building an investment portfolio. A related question is, what percentage of a family's disposable income should go into equities? Disposable income, in this sense, is money one can afford to spend without impairing one's basic budget or encroaching on a prudent reserve for such emergencies as illness or loss of income.

The decision as to how much of one's savings to commit to common stocks must vary with the individual. An elderly widow, an affluent professional man, and a newly married blue-collar worker, for example, have different needs. Depending upon the margin of safety required by

your own financial and family situation, your
common stock holdings may vary from 25 to 75
percent of your investment holdings.

Although they operate on a much larger scale,
managers of pension funds or college endowments
must cope with essentially the same investment
problems as the individual: to preserve capital
while seeking to increase the original stake and
obtain greater future income. You can solve those
problems the way the professionals do. Once you
have created a base of solid income in savings
accounts, government bonds, and high-grade corporate bonds, you can afford to put some money
at risk in common stocks that promise growth of
capital.

If you already own stocks or have decided to
invest in them, you have another decision to
make: How will you invest? Should you buy
stocks on your own or use one of the group investment methods described later in this book,
such as a mutual fund, a closed-end investment
company, an investment club, or a variable
annuity?

This chapter describes the techniques of solo
investing used by experienced investors to select
specific stocks for purchase. Two basic schools of
stock market analysis are used to decide when to
buy and sell:

Fundamentals.

This approach gives close attention to the economic outlook for an industry and the companies
it comprises. You project a promising company's
earnings (see Chapter 7) and capitalize those
earnings at a realistic rate. This gives an intrinsic
value, which can be compared to the existing

market price. Then you can decide whether the stock is a buy—underpriced enough to allow a potential for profit.

Technical.

This approach assumes that "everybody knows more than anybody," and that the ticker tape tells you what everybody knows, or believes, about the market. The technical analyst—the chartist, as Wall Street calls him—finds on the ticker the trends caused by the interaction of supply and demand, market volume, emotional factors, public psychology, the business climate, and news developments. His basic assumption is that what has happened before will happen again.

One of the most successful long-run managers of a series of mutual funds keeps a staff of fundamentalists and one of chartists. When their recommendations cross, as he calls it, he feels he has a buy or sell signal. Actually, most investors freely mingle fundamental and technical analysis in making stock market judgments. The main thrust of this book, however, is on fundamentals, not on the market maneuvers by which traders seek to make money out of buying and selling to one another. Disregard of fundamental and realistic values frequently leads investors into the expensive errors of "Games Investors Play," as described by Shearson Hayden Stone, a leading securities firm:

> *Follow the Leader.* A popular game, although professionals rarely play it. The object is to find out what everyone else is buying, then buy it. The player loses when he arrives at the starting point too late, which is inevitable under the rules.

Yo-Yo. Played by investors who believe that
every stock which goes down must inevitably
come back again. This game takes patience
while the investor waits to recoup his losses.
The player loses when he sticks to a dud instead of switching to a more promising stock.

I Love You, I Love You. Common among
emotional investors. The player falls in love
with a stock that has brought him paper
profits, although it has stagnated recently.
He looks upon it as a faithful old friend . . .
a costly form of anthropomorphism.

As an investor you must avoid letting emotions
affect decisions. There must be logical business
reasons for every move you make or do not make.
For example, when cash savings and bonds offer
higher returns than dividends on stocks and require little attention, why consider stocks with
their fluctuations and risks at all?

One good business reason, in addition to the
hope of capital gains, may be tax advantages:

1. As noted in Chapter 18, the first $200 of
dividends a married couple receives from stocks
each year is completely tax-exempt.

2. Gains on shares which you sell after owning
them for more than nine months are taxed at the
long-term capital gains rate. In most cases only
half the gains are added to your regular income
and taxed at your top bracket.

3. Any excess of losses over gains may be partly
deductible from other income, such as salary (within limits described in Chapter 18).

**Diversification
in Solo
Investing**

As an investor in the stock market, you must

be prepared to devote time and effort to research and continuing review of the shares you accumulate. Even though your portfolio is not big, it will require almost daily attention.

Another requirement of successful investing in common stocks is enough capital to diversify your investment in at least three or four different companies. This enables you to avoid committing all your funds at one time or in one stock. A prudent investor never risks all his capital on the future course of the market. It is difficult to achieve even moderate diversification without an initial investment of at least $4,000-$5,000. Investing in only one or two stocks heightens the chance that unforeseen events could cost you money. Even a blue chip such as AT&T, the favorite stock of small investors, lost much of its value in the late 1960s and in 1970.

If you decide to buy stocks on your own, there are several methods of reducing the risks. One is "dollar averaging." Dollar averaging can level out the fluctuations of the market in a particular stock, especially if the stock is in a volatile or cyclical industry. Dollar averaging enables you to minimize the importance of timing and to avoid the dangers of attempting to second-guess the market.

Here is how dollar averaging works: Suppose you decide to invest $1,800 in a certain stock. Instead of investing the entire sum at one time, you plan to invest $600 every four months for one year. During periods when the stock's price declines, your $600 buys more shares. When the price rises, your $600 buys fewer shares. Over the long term you accumulate your shares at an average price.

If, for example, your stock sells for $30 at the

beginning, your initial $600 purchase buys 20 shares. If the price four months later drops to $20, your second $600 buys 30 shares. If the price in the third period climbs to $40, your $600 buys 15 shares. And even though the average price of the shares in those three periods was $30, your stock purchases (because you bought more shares for your $600 at $20 a share) averaged $27.69 a share.

While dollar averaging enables you to reduce the risks of bad timing, you lose the opportunity to buy at low points for big gains. However, even partially accurate timing requires a close watch on market trends (as discussed in Chapter 4) and is seldom achieved even by professional traders. For the investor who seeks to minimize risks, is unable to spend time watching the market signals, and is willing to settle for a small potential gain over the longer period, the trade-off is a fair one.

Dollar averaging was the cornerstone of the NYSE's Monthly Investment Plan, which was instituted in 1954 to allow everyone to own a share of American industry. The small investor could accumulate stock on a regular basis, with payments as low as $40 monthly or even quarterly.

By the beginning of 1973, there were about 335,000 MIP plans. Then a period set in during which "shares of American industry" were selling at disastrous discounts and MIP members were selling out at the bottom like other small investors.

In April, 1976, the Big Board finally abandoned MIP, but it was more of a transfer than a disappearance. Merrill Lynch, which had always handled most MIP accounts, merged MIP with its so-called Sharebuilder Plan. A Sharebuilder account allows the customer to invest any amount he chooses in any of the stocks listed on the New York Stock Exchange or American Stock Exchange or in any of 500 substantial over-the-counter stocks in which Merrill Lynch is a market maker. There are 400,000 Sharebuilder accounts on Merrill Lynch's books; no breakdown of those that were originally from the Monthly Investment Plan is kept.

The absence of an odd-lot differential, and discounts from previously enforced standard commissions, have reduced the costs of building a stock portfolio by monthly payments. Critics of the former MIP always stressed the extra charges that brokers had to make to be able to handle MIP accounts. The criticisms echoed those made against Christmas Clubs and level-payment life insurance policies. On paper, it can be proved that those methods of forced savings are extravagantly expensive; in practice, the Christmas Club member and the level-payment policyholder, come Christmas or retirement age, are likely to have money the critic lacks.

You do pay substantially higher brokerage rates on investments under $100 than if you accumulate cash and then buy stocks with a lump sum. You can reduce this cost by investing a larger amount quarterly, or even twice a year, and still achieve the benefits of dollar averaging. You can work out your own version of such a periodic stock accumulation plan.

Another way to achieve some diversification with small investments is to buy shares in companies that own stock in other companies and in mortgages and real estate. Among these are banks, **Other Ways to Spread the Risk**

insurance companies, and the "closed-end" investment companies described in Chapter 10.

An interesting and often educational way to
obtain diversification is through an investment
club. In an investment club, members of professional, fraternal or social organizations, groups of
friends, or even families agree to put up so many
dollars a month. By banding together, they achieve
many of the benefits available only to large investors. They buy in round lots, thus paying lower
commissions; they share, in manageable pieces,
the job of looking for good investments; and because they manage a sizeable investment account,
they are given more attention and assistance by
brokers and company executives.

There are 60,000 such clubs. About 14,000 are
members of the National Association of Investment Clubs. Membership in the NAIC costs $10
a year for the group, plus $1.50 for each member
who subscribes to *Better Investing*, the association's magazine. Most clubs consist of ten to
twenty members who meet once a month and invest about $25 a month per member.

NAIC, or a broker experienced in advising investment clubs, can explain the different kinds of
agreements used to form clubs. A partnership
usually has tax advantages for moderate income
investors, while an incorporated club may be more
useful for upper bracket taxpayers. You can also
combine several of these media. Many investment
club members also buy stocks and mutual funds on
their own.

Investment   Investment counselors and brokers usually
Objectives   classify stocks according to the investor's needs

and objectives. The following groupings illustrate:

• High-quality or blue chip stocks are the foundation of a good portfolio. The companies are established industry leaders with a history of growth in both earnings and dividends.

• Growth stocks are for the investor who wants above-average growth and is willing to assume above-average risks to achieve it. Income is not a factor, since most growth stocks yield about 1 percent or less.

• Income stocks are chosen for high immediate yield and stability of principal, forgoing any but minor capital gains.

• Special situation stocks are chosen periodically for various reasons, most of which, it is felt, will result in improved profits and higher stock prices. For example, a company may terminate a venture that had been losing money.

Although most brokers and advisory services offer lists of stocks classified according to some such objectives, such classification should not be taken too literally. There are many overlaps and exceptions.

Also, the distinction between speculation and investing is less clear these days. Income stocks such as public utilities may suffer sharp price declines during periods of rising interest rates although the dividends are usually assured. At other times, such stocks may offer potential growth as well as good current yields.

Guides to Value

As an investor, you must constantly bear in mind that the future is unknown to all, even the experts. You cannot buy just any stock and expect to be guaranteed a share of the gains from a rising market. The averages may go up while your stock declines. Of fifty industries tracked by Johnson's Charts from 1967-76, the average gain was 53 percent. However, only nineteen of the industries performed above the average. Of the thirty-one remaining industries, thirteen declined.

The investor's primary task is to look for good value, using as his basic criterion the price at which the stock is selling compared with its earnings and the prospect for further growth of these earnings. This yardstick is called the "price-earnings" ratio (P/E). The P/E figures—stock market price compared with the company's latest twelve-month earnings-per-share of stock outstanding—are reported in financial reference works such as *Moody's Handbook* and Data Digests' *Monthly Stock Digest*. These can be found in libraries and in brokers' offices.

To calculate the price-earnings ratio, divide the annual earnings into the market price of the stock. A stock selling for $28 and earning $2 a share net (after taxes) has a P/E of 14. The P/E usually influences investor interest in a stock more than the dividend rate and thus affects the price at which the stock sells.

However, older persons with a need for immediate income will be more interested in the dividend rate. The dividend rate is calculated by dividing the stock's market price into its annual dividend. A stock selling at $40 and paying a $1.20 dividend would have a dividend rate, or yield, of 3 percent.

A high dividend rate does not necessarily signal good value. The yield may be high because of a relatively high "payout rate." Some corporations pay out as much as 70 percent of their earnings

in dividends. Others pay very little. Growth companies tend to pay less dividends, preferring
instead to plow earnings back into research and
expansion.

While investors nowadays give greater emphasis to growth, a high dividend, if the company is
able to sustain it, is in itself a form of growth.
Such returns can be reinvested and compounded.
And in times of declining or sideways markets,
stocks which pay high dividends make waiting for
recovery more tolerable. Nor is it necessarily true
that high dividend payers are greater risks. Like
all stocks, their investment quality varies according to their productivity and earnings.

Long-Term Capital Gains

The reason many investors prefer stocks with
growth potential to stocks that merely provide high
dividends is that the growth stock promises long-
term capital gains.

By definition, a serious investor is a person who
has more than enough income to satisfy his wants.
And he pays enough in taxes that the capital-gains
tax advantage over the tax on his ordinary income
is substantial.

The arithmetic is simple. If stocks as a group are
selling at 12 times earnings and pay 5 percent dividends, a stock earning $1 a year, with no prospect
of earning more any time soon, will sell for $12 and
pay 60 cents.

Assume that another stock is confidently expected to increase its present $1 a year earnings by
10 percent a year. Five years hence it will be earning $1.60 a share and selling for $19. The investor
will make the same 5 percent a year he is getting
from the stodgy stock by paying 14½ for the

How Different Groups of Stocks
Compare in Price, Earnings & Dividends

	Price *Feb. 28, 1977*
HIGH QUALITY OR BLUE CHIP STOCKS	
Campbell Soup	$ 38½
Citicorp	29
Dow Chemical	36⅞
Exxon	50⅞
Ford Motor	57⅞
General Electric	50½
General Foods	32⅛
General Motors	70¾
International Paper	56⅛
Kraftco	44
R. J. Reynolds	65½
Safeway Stores	47⅛
Standard Oil (Indiana)	52¼
Union Oil of California	57¼
GROWTH STOCKS	
American Home Products	30⅞
Avon Products	44⅝
Baxter Laboratories	32¼
Bristol-Myers	63⅜
Coca-Cola	76⅝
Eastman Kodak	74⅜
International Business Machines	276
J.C. Penney	40¾
Procter & Gamble	82⅜
Sears, Roebuck	63
Xerox	50⅜
PUBLIC UTILITY INCOME STOCKS	
American Telephone & Telegraph	63⅝
Commonwealth Edison	29⅞
Duke Power Company	20⅜
Gulf States Utilities	13⅝
Indianapolis Power & Light	23¾
Long Island Lighting	18½
New England Electric System	22¼
Southern California Edison	21⅝
Union Electric	15½
CYCLICAL STOCKS	
Beckman Instruments	23⅞
Eastern Gas & Fuel	26⅛
Joy Manufacturing	43⅞
Louisiana Pacific	15
NCR Corporation	35½
Raytheon	57¼
Southern Railway	55¾

Earnings 1976	Price- Earnings Ratio	Annual Dividend Rate	Yield (percent)
$ 3.19	12	$1.36	3.8%
3.24	9	.94	3.3
3.30	11	.90	2.7
5.90	9	2.72½	5.9
10.45	6	2.80	5.5
4.12	12	1.65	3.6
3.45	12	1.50	5.1
10.08	7	5.55	7.8
5.60	10	2.00	3.5
4.86	9	2.12	5.3
7.48	9	3.13	5.0
4.07	12	2.05	4.6
6.09	9	2.30	5.0
7.42	8	2.07	3.7
1.75	18	1.00	3.6
2.90	15	1.80	4.5
1.85	17	.21¾	.7
4.90	13	1.80	3.5
4.57	16	2.65	3.5
4.03	18	2.06	2.8
15.94	17	8.00	3.6
3.74	11	1.25	3.1
5.38	15	2.15	3.2
3.92	14	1.85	3.3
4.51	11	1.05	2.4
6.05	11	3.70	6.6
3.24	9	2.37½	8.0
2.40	8	1.52½	7.9
1.54	9	1.12	8.2
2.52	9	1.82	8.0
2.52	7	1.54½	8.4
2.53	9	1.84	8.4
3.70	6	1.68	7.8
1.86	8	1.34	8.8
1.67	14	.28	1.3
3.01	9	.67	3.1
3.79	12	1.15	3.0
1.51	10	.20	1.3
3.53	10	.72	2.3
5.58	10	1.10	2.1
5.85	10	2.27	4.2

Source: Standard & Poor's Corporation

growth stock and holding it five years. Moreover, his tax bill will be cut roughly in half.

If the growth stock is expected to gain earnings at the tremendous rate of 20 percent a year, the five-year projection is for earnings to reach $2.50 a share and the price $30. Still assuming that 5 percent is a satisfactory dividend, the investor would be justified in paying $23 today for the shares of stock.

Possible Dangers   As investors periodically discover, there are many ifs in such calculations. The growth stock may show a decline in its rate of growth, either as its early successes fill the first eager demand, or as competitors are drawn into its field.

The interest rate which translates future growth into present value may change. After all, in recent periods much less than five years has been required to see interest of Treasury bills, nearest to cash of any investment, move from below 4 percent to above 9 percent.

Gravest danger of all, the growth stock's very success may attract so many buyers that the price runs past the indicated value. Sudden price declines have occurred in the past, and will recur in the future, when long-term holders decide that the time has come to cash in.

The investor's protection against that kind of disappointment is to do his own arithmetic; the customer's man or the stockbroker's analyst will not do it for him. Better to lose the last few dollars of profit on a growth stock than to hold on to it too long.

Often brokers and counselors recommend blue chip or generally accepted growth companies de-

spite their high P/Es. This is almost a self-fulfilling
estimate: as long as the "Nifty Fifty" stocks, as
Wall Street calls these favorites, *are* favorites in so
many portfolios, there will be a market for them.
But the Nifty Fifty shares will go down with all the
others in a bear market.

Other stocks may be selling at lower P/Es than
their earnings and prospects merit either because
of a temporary interruption in their normal
growth or because they are temporarily out of
fashion.

The goal of research-minded investors is to find
stocks with moderate P/E ratios and reasonably
sound future prospects. Opportunities exist because the market's evaluation of specific stocks is
sometimes affected by faddism. There is not always a valid business reason for the very sharp
differences in market valuation of stocks of the
same growth character, with P/E ratios ranging
from 12 to 40. A stock may sell one year for 15
times earnings and the next year for 25 times
earnings with no significant change in its earnings trend.

An example of how bandwagon psychology can
affect the price of a stock beyond any valid reason
for the fluctuation can be seen in what happened
to the common stock of Bausch & Lomb. In 1970
the lens manufacturer's shares sold for as high
as $79 and as low as $27, all on the same twelve-
months' earnings of $1.56 a share, with a divi-
dend of 80 cents a share. These prices represented
a P/E of 51 at the high for the year and 17 at
the low.

Then in 1971 the company announced a newly-
developed "soft" contact lens. The stock soared all
the way to $147, a P/E of 94. But there was still

no change in earnings or dividends. Prospective higher earnings and dividends were discounted far into the future. The late buyers who did not stop to assess the real value and real prospects lost heavily. Within weeks of reaching its $147 peak, the price of the stock had dropped to $106. The slide continued through 1972. Near year's end, Bausch & Lomb traded around 22, for a P/E of 13—much lower than it had ever sold before the soft lens was heard of. Some Wall Street observers saw signs that significant buying was coming into the stock at that level.

Selection Difficult   Finding stocks with reasonable P/E ratios is not difficult. There are hundreds listed in stock market reference works such as Standard & Poor's or Moody's. Evaluating their future prospects requires more research and experience. Even professional analysts have difficulty selecting stocks that will outperform the market averages.

You really need to compare recommendations from several sources and then decide on the basis of your own convictions.

Your first task is to determine the company's earnings trend for at least four or five years to see whether it actually has been able to increase earnings and at what rate. A genuine growth stock is considered to be one that has increased earnings by 10 percent a year. A lower growth rate may be a rewarding long-term investment if the price is correspondingly lower and the yield relatively high.

Often industries and individual stocks have what is described as a "normal" P/E. For example, professional investors may feel that the accepted P/E of an industry or company lies between 10 and 12. You can determine the typical range of P/E valuation for stock or industry by consulting a broker or checking through Moody's or Data Digests for several past years. Often, undervalued stocks can be found among companies and industries currently out of vogue among professional investors. Such stocks, however, may meet resistance for a time in pushing through the barriers of "normal" valuation, unless new developments or good news changes the investment industry's concept of their worth.

It cannot be said too often that P/E ratios must be judged in view of the whole market. When the P/E of a broad group like the Standard & Poor's 500 stocks falls from 18 to 8, the fact that the P/E of a market favorite has moved from 20 to 12 is hardly a buy signal. Keeping an eye on a stock's P/E is still a sound practice; when the P/E of a sound stock has gone below its usual ratio to that of stocks in general, take a close look. Have fundamentals, in the company or the industry, changed, or is it a case of neglect while the fickle market chases a fad?

There are groups of stocks that command high multiples because of assumed resistance to bad economic news. Some have low multiples because their markets dry up in hard times. When the first group becomes too dear it may be time to sell. When the second group gets too low it may be time to buy. Rather, it is time to study the individual stock; it is never the right time to buy or sell stock by rigid formula.

The individual who can invest in several companies at the start can balance his initial effort by the selection of one or two "income" stocks.

While some growth stocks are priced higher at times than many conservative investment managers feel they are worth, there are possible selections among some of the less prominent, medium-grade and smaller growth stocks and among those that may just miss the growth classification but have shown fairly consistent earnings gains of over 5 percent a year.

Smaller or young growth companies usually sell at lower multiples, and a product or technology breakthrough can affect their earnings more drastically than in the case of large companies. Such companies, however, need close scrutiny, especially in the case of new or unseasoned issues, as discussed in Chapter 9.

How much are stocks in general worth? In periods of stock market booms, the P/E ratio of the widely used stock averages had multiples of 20 to 25. At those times so-called growth stocks sold for 30 to 90 times earnings.

In recent years the averages have dropped below 10 in market declines before recovering. Here are P/E ratios of the Dow-Jones industrial average in recent years, taking the midway period of the year: 1963, 18 times combined earnings of the stocks comprising the average; '64, 19; '65, 16; '66, 14; '67, 17; '68, 18; '69, 14; '70, 15; '71, 15; '72, 16; '73, 11.5; '74, 10.4; '75, 10.5; '76, 9.6.

Note that the stocks comprising the Dow-Jones are "blue chips." The broader Standard & Poor's indexes show greater swings.

The long-term P/E trend has been downward all through the 1961-70 decade. In the intermediate trends, recovery usually starts within three to six months. The average high in recent years has been 17 times earnings; the average low, 14.

In trying to predict prices of stocks, professional money managers consider the prospects of both the industry and the individual company. It is not enough to determine that a company is part of a successful industry or has good prospects or has enjoyed favorable news recently. For example, not all companies involved in computer technology have been successful. Each company should be considered on its own merits.

Evaluating Future Prospects

Among the factors money managers consider when evaluating future prospects are where and why the industry and the specific company can be expected to grow, the return it has been able to earn on its invested capital, its profit margin, and its predicted future earnings. Brokers' analysts often visit company plants and offices and obtain on-the-spot information about future prospects. They make these reports available to customers.

Some investors make their own evaluations of a company's prospects. They talk to dealers and users of the company's products to determine their experience and satisfaction.

It is harder to judge the quality of management. Among the yardsticks used by professional analysts to judge management effectiveness are the following: its recent earnings record; its relations with personnel and customers; the opinions of other people in the same business; whether it employs its capital fully or holds large amounts of semi-idle cash; how active it is in research and development of new products or new uses for its present products; and its awareness of new trends that may affect its profitability.

Related Opportunities   Often when an expanding industry attracts investor interest, but shares in its companies jump sharply, experienced investors will turn to the companies that supply the industry or to sellers of related products and services.

However, there is a danger in overvaluing the prospects of related companies. After the boom in stocks of computer manufacturing companies, many investors bought shares in independent companies manufacturing peripheral equipment and computer software. The stocks of these companies went up sharply, and in 1970 came down just as fast. One of the leading manufacturers of peripheral equipment was even charged by the Securities and Exchange Commission with issuing inflated earnings reports.

Special and Turnaround Situations   Professional analysts constantly seek "special situations." These may be companies with new opportunities, such as those with stakes in the recent expansion of health and education facilities. But often they are companies which have had uneven records of mediocre performances, but have new potential for appreciation. Sometimes they are cyclical. For example, capital-goods, machine-tool, and construction companies benefit from periodic upswings.

However, special situations need to be appraised realistically. Brokers and advisory services often publish lists of such special situations. Sometimes many stocks on these lists already have risen appreciably by the time they are published. Others may still have reasonable P/Es.

CHAPTER 3

Buying Stocks for Income

The only practical reason for investing in common stocks is that some day they will be worth more than you the investor paid for them. Higher immediate yields are always available from savings accounts and bonds. However, in these inflationary days, some investors, whose income and tax positions would seem to guide them exclusively toward high-income securities, buy common stocks as a hedge against inflation.

These investors generally direct their attention to the "defensive" stocks. These are stocks whose shares—in price and in yield—are best able to resist recessions. This may be because their returns are virtually guaranteed, as is the case with public utilities, or because they make and sell

Stock Prices vs. the Rising Cost of Living

1967 = 100

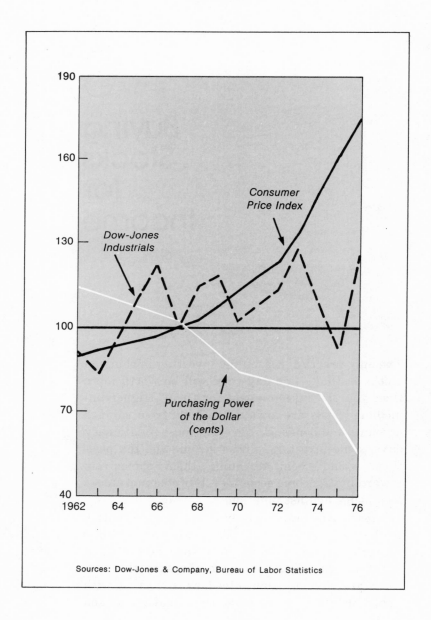

Sources: Dow-Jones & Company, Bureau of Labor Statistics

basic daily necessities. Food and drug companies are included in the defensive category on this basis.

At the opposite end of the scale from defensive industries are cyclical companies. These range from automobile and appliance manufacturers, purchases of which can be postponed as incomes fall, to the metal producing, heavy manufacturing and construction fields, for whose wares there may be literally no market at all for long stretches of time. Some Wall Streeters detect the unerring signal of a bear market on the day that all the copper stocks reach new highs. The reasoning is that copper companies show their best earnings just when the market for new plant and office buildings reaches the saturation point.

Experienced investors who are primarily interested in growth often try to balance their portfolios with good defensive stocks. Such balance is especially useful to the small investor who depends on his portfolio for a substantial part of his current income.

Defensive stocks often pay high dividends. In addition, some have growth characteristics. Into this category fall food processors and retailers; drug companies; hospital supply and equipment manufacturers; fuel and utility companies; banks and shoe companies. At times the stocks of some insurance, oil, and finance companies are also classified as defensive.

Utilities such as electric, telephone, and natural gas companies are favorites of small investors. As noted earlier, AT&T is the most widely purchased stock. Utility stocks provide dependable income and sometimes offer moderate growth in areas of expanding population. But as many investors learned during the late 1960s, the prices of utility shares become unstable in periods of tight money and high interest rates.

Utilities have long been regarded as "income" investments—a piece of conventional wisdom that may have to be discarded with some others if inflation cannot be kept within bounds. When interest rates are high, the bonds of utilities, which are always building, must pay the going rates. In such cases the prices of their shares must fall until they yield as much as the bonds—minus, perhaps, a small premium for future growth. In late 1974 the common shares of a well-regarded Eastern utility were paying a 13 percent return, stocks of utilities in the high-growth Southwest could be had to yield 9.5 percent, and even mighty AT&T's shares were priced to yield 7.3 percent.

When interest rates decline, utility stocks usually rise to a level where experienced investors sell them. When AT&T sold for $75 in the 1960s, it yielded only 3 percent. And that $75 price was the peak from which a six-year decline began.

It is also wise to keep abreast of developments that may alter a company's outlook. Consolidated Edison of New York, chiefly a supplier of electricity, once relied on cheap Venezuelan fuel oil. A sharp rise in the price of oil, an even more costly requirement for upgrading the oil used in terms of lower emissions of pollutants, and the refusal of regulatory bodies to grant offsetting rate increases found Con Edison passing a dividend in 1974. The stock, which had sold as high as $49 in the 1960s and reached what many would have guessed to be an all-time low of $22 in 1970, plunged to $6 a share.

The investor who reasoned at that time that regulators must eventually bow to arithmetic would have seen his $6 shares rise to $23 by the end of 1976. At the current $22.50, the $2 dividend returns nearly 9 percent, yet Con Edison's P/E is still only 5! Courage and common sense can often lead to wise investments while the stock market technicians are running for cover.

Long-term bonds of utilities were cited earlier as alternatives to utility common stocks for the investor seeking high current yield. In ordinary times, whenever yields on common stocks match those of bonds, a buying opportunity has arrived; the buyer gets growth potential for nothing. In extraordinary times such as the summer of 1974, with common stocks paying more than bonds, the prudent small investor will stay on the sidelines.

It has been profitable in the past to compare price-earnings ratios of common-stock averages and the averages for electric utilities. When the P/E average for utilities is considerably lower, professional investors move into utilities. This rule should not be followed blindly. In August, 1974, Moody's Industrials (an average of leading industrial stocks) had a P/E ratio of 10.6; Moody's Electric Utilities had one of 6.6. Investors were declaring their disbelief in the reality of reported industrial earnings, and their doubt that utilities would escape from the inflation trap soon. Neither mood is one in which to invest.

It should be noted that the utilities fall into two groups of widely differing prospects. In growing areas like the South, the Southwest, and some of the Plains States, utilities' P/E ratios will continue to be higher than those of older metropolitan areas.

The reasons are simple. In Arizona or Florida the voters—which in turn means the regulatory officials—still give primacy to growth. The land

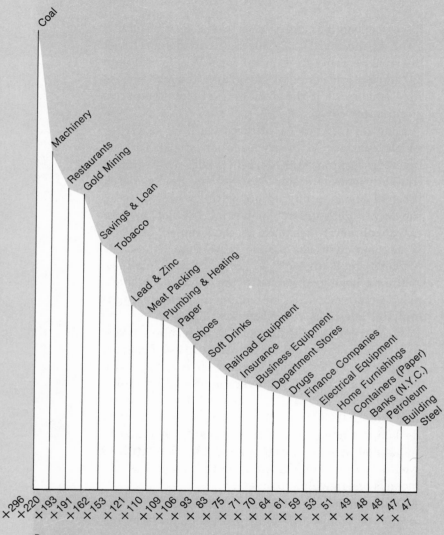

Coal

Machinery

Restaurants

Gold Mining

Savings & Loan

Tobacco

Lead & Zinc

Meat Packing

Plumbing & Heating

Paper

Shoes

Soft Drinks

Railroad Equipment

Insurance

Business Equipment

Department Stores

Drugs

Finance Companies

Electrical Equipment

Home Furnishings

Containers (Paper)

Banks (N.Y.C.)

Petroleum

Building

Steel

+296 +220 +193 +191 +162 +153 +121 +110 +109 +106 +93 +83 +75 +71 +70 +64 +61 +59 +53 +51 +49 +48 +48 +47 +47
× ×

*Percentage
Gain or Loss*

Source: Johnson's Charts

How Stocks of 50 Industries Performed
Over 10-Year Period, end-1966 to end-1976

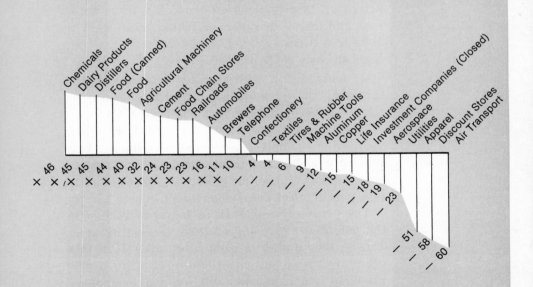

still affords room for plants, and power lines are viewed with pride rather than disgust.

But, in the cities, too many people—from the utilities' standpoint—occupy themselves with the environment. Consolidated Edison of New York cannot build a plant on the Hudson River because it would endanger fish. While the courts adjudicate that contention, construction costs keep rising and overloaded equipment keeps breaking down.

Another defensive investment is bank stocks. Banks are in a protected position because much of their income is derived from their own investments in high-quality bonds. These stocks often have growth quality as well, even more than utilities. Banks have an earnings advantage when money is tight because interest rates are high. On the other hand, they also thrive when money is plentiful because they can increase their lending activities. In a rare period of stock market weakness and broad loan demand, bank stocks went in 1974 to a 9 percent yield basis. Most of the time bank stocks yield 5 or 6 percent.

In looking for high-yielding defensive stocks that also may have moderate growth characteristics, an experienced investor will review the earnings of several stocks for the past five or ten years. For example, a local electric company that currently yields 7 percent and has been able to show at least an average 3 percent growth in earnings over the last decade has a foot in both camps.

The prospective growth of banks is related to the potential expansion of their marketing area. Among food and drug companies, growth factors often are connected with the development of new products and expansion into related businesses.

Food and drug sales and earnings generally tend to grow only in accordance with population growth.

Some factors to consider include your estimate of potential growth. Is there room for further residential business and industrial expansion in the utility's service area? Other important questions are whether management has been able to keep the company and its equipment operating efficiently and whether it has reasonably harmonious relations with its employees and the communities it serves. In addition, it is important to note whether the industry has any severe ecological problems.

4

Timing
Investments

Although fundamental value and long-term growth are of overriding importance to the true investor, as distinguished from the in-and-out trader, he would have to be more or less than human if he did not rejoice over purchasing a stock at a substantially lower price than the one quoted in the stock market tables or lament buying at a substantially higher price.

An understanding of the technical factors that govern the movements of the market can help the investor increase his gains and minimize his losses. Charles H. Dow, the first man to attempt serious technical analysis of the market's movements, wrote:

The market always has three movements, all

going on at the same time. The first is the
narrow movement from day to day. The second is the short swing, running from two
weeks to a month or more. The third is the
main move . . .

Dow and his disciples—S. A. Nelson, who first
christened the Dow Theory in 1902, and William
Peter Hamilton, a long-time editor of the Wall
Street Journal—considered it impractical to follow the shorter movements. They contended that
the principal value of the Dow Theory lay in pre-
dicting the course of business over the next few
years, rather than in helping the investor reap
profits.

The Dow Theory divides the market into categories of industry and transportation and originally kept track of the performance of twelve
selected "blue chip" industrial stocks and a similar selection of twenty railroad stocks. Today,
truck and airline stocks have been added, and
the number of industrials has risen to thirty. According to Dow Theory technicians, the market is
in a basic upward trend if one of these averages
advances above a previous important high, accom-
panied or followed by a similar advance in the
other. When the averages of both categories dip
below previous important lows, this is regarded
as confirmation of a basic downtrend.

The Dow Theory made sense when railroads
were the only mode of commercial transport, and
companies were owned by the men who ran them.
The market reflected the beliefs of men who had
the power to take action that would make their
hopes come true. In today's vastly expanded market, those people are in the minority.

Nevertheless, the Dow Theory still influences
the market, if only because people expect other
people to act upon it. It has given rise, moreover,
to dozens of attempts to fathom shifts in investor
psychology—the hopes and fears, wisdom and
folly, of all the people who bring their shares or
their money to the auction market.

A popular signal—hinted at by Dow but re-
jected by Hamilton—is the double top or double
bottom. Often stocks will reach a peak, fall off a
little, then return to the earlier figure but fail to
go above it. Technicians say the last hopeful buyer
who has entered the market must be growing less
hopeful and will soon be ready to lead a retreat
into cash, thus starting a major downturn. Conversely, a double bottom means that the last die-
hard loser has taken his losses; the next move
will find the market full of buyers and devoid of
sellers.

Professional investors also look for the technical indicators known as support and resistance
zones. A support zone marks the point at which
buying interest previously developed and stocks
started upward. The violation of a support zone
indicates that a considerable further drop is in
prospect. Conversely, a resistance zone marks the
general price level at which a previous rise ended.
A breakthrough indicates an unsatisfied appetite
for shares.

One technical indicator, widely used but of dubious value, is odd-lot trading. Figures are supplied
each day on the purchase and sale of odd lots—
shares in less than multiples of 100. These show
whether small traders believe the market will go
up or down. The reasoning is that small traders
are usually wrong. According to the theory they

tend to buy at the peak of a bull market, just before the downturn, and sell when the market is low and professional investors begin to buy up bargains.

When odd-lot sales exceed purchases by more than 10 percent, the theory goes, it is a signal to buy. Conversely, a sell signal is indicated when odd-lot buying exceeds sales for a number of months. Odd-lot figures, however, are becoming increasingly difficult to interpret, perhaps because small investors are becoming more sophisticated. For example, odd-lot buying was conspicuous in the 1971 upturn of stock values. Moreover, the whole community of in-and-out traders loses on balance; if the odd-lotter is wrong, he is wrong just a little sooner than his larger fellows.

Thomas F. Woodlock wrote on March 16, 1945:

> Brokers' offices are always full of stocks after a large rise in prices and bare of stocks at the end of a long fall. They came from the [investors'] strongboxes and they went back to them. The speculators bought on the rising markets and sold on the falling ones; [the investors] sold on rising markets and bought on falling ones.

For the investor who follows the market closely —and remember that the investor wins what the speculator loses—there are common sense signs indicating that stocks in general are approaching their highs. One is the average yield of industrial stocks in comparison to yields in other securities. Yields on stocks drop as their prices rise. When yields on corporate, municipal, and government bonds and other investment media rise well above stock yields, you can expect investment funds to flow out of the stock market.

Another sign that a bull market may be nearing its end is when the average price-earnings ratio of many stocks, or of the Dow-Jones list of industrials, reaches significantly higher than normal levels.

The volume of trading is a third signal. When the volume of sales on the exchanges tends to increase on days when prices are falling and fall when prices are rising, this indicates that other investors are becoming cautious and may soon sell out. Shrinking volume itself may be another clue to a mature bull market.

A fourth signal of an imminent downturn is increased speculation on new issues of relatively unknown companies while established stocks and stable dividend payers are tending to fall in price. Increased speculation in shares on the more speculative American Stock Exchange may signal a general drop. For example, while the price-earnings multiple for the Dow-Jones average of leading issues traded on the New York Stock Exchange gradually moved down from 18 in 1964 to 15 in 1969, the median price-earnings figure on the American Exchange doubled from 13 to 26 in the same time. The average price-earnings multiple was actually 40.

Bellwether Stocks   Some market observers follow the actions of what they call "bellwether stocks" in order to forecast future ups and downs. Probably the most important of these is General Motors, which generally has been an accurate and leading indicator of the Dow-Jones industrial average. GM watchers claim that investors can expect a continued upturn as long as this stock is advancing. Similarly, if GM is in a declining trend, they see this as a signal for caution. Jacques Coe, a successful underwriter, once said that no bull market could survive fifty sessions in which GM did not reach a new high.

Another set of general indicators are the cyclical or seasonal trends. These, as analyzed by the Wright Investors' Service over a ten-year period, are as follows:

Seasonal Trends

• The Spring Rise usually begins early in March and often lasts until mid-May.

• The Summer Rally generally follows price weakness prior to vacation period and is likely (but not always) to begin during the last week in June and extend through July.

• The Autumn Sell-Off begins any time after Labor Day and gains strength in mid-October, particularly in a declining market. It reflects, in part, advance tax loss sales in anticipation of later repurchase under the thirty-one-day rule.

• The Year-End Advance generally gets under way during the last week in October. It has averaged a 6 percent rise in good years and a 7 percent rise in bear-market years.

The investor must never lose sight of the fact that all technical indicators, even the sophisticated methods used by professionals, are imprecise and cannot be used to pinpoint the bottoms and tops of the market. Some investors make it a policy to sell on the way up, reducing their holdings while still maintaining some stake in a further rise. They also try to eliminate some of their less successful holdings or those whose prospects do not appear particularly bright.

Small investors can adapt the techniques of formula investing such as dollar averaging. By this means, you can insure a degree of protection against losses caused by unforeseen market swings and possibly use these swings to your advantage.

As explained in Chapter 2, dollar averaging is the investment of the same dollar amount in a stock at regular intervals—monthly, quarterly, or annually. This enables you to buy more shares when the price is low and less when the price is high. Mutual funds are ideally suited to dollar averaging because they allow reinvestment of dividends and capital gains without additional commissions.

Another formula used to diminish the risk of stock fluctuation is the constant-dollar plan. Here the investor divides his money—say, $20,000— into stocks and bonds or some other fixed security paying a high yield. He puts $10,000 into stocks. If the market goes up 20 percent, stocks are sold to bring the stock account back to $10,000. If prices fall 20 percent, funds are transferred from the bond portion to build the stocks up to $10,000.

A variation of the constant-dollar plan is the constant ratio formula, which calls for a 50-50 ratio between stocks and bonds. If the market rises 20 percent, stocks are sold and bonds are bought to restore the 50-50 ratio. This plan enables the investor to keep more of his funds in stocks during a rising market, instead of being limited to the fixed dollar amount. This formula is flexible, allowing the investor, for instance, to keep 70 percent of his funds in stocks and 30 percent in fixed securities.

In general, formulas should not be "followed out the window." Instead, they should be used as yardsticks for adjusting a portfolio against probable market moves and maintaining a strong financial position under all circumstances.

Fluctuations in the stock market often exaggerate general economic trends and sometimes give false signals. However, when the market does anticipate accurately, it usually does so four to six months in advance of the general decline or recovery.

Sometimes a stock you own may seem to fluctuate unduly, although the market in general is relatively quiet. In that case, ask your broker or consult the various financial publications to see if any adverse news has developed in the company or in the industry.

When you do incur losses in a stock, conventional Wall Street wisdom advises you to cut your losses quickly—do not let them ride. Some professional analysts suggest that near-term traders get out if the loss is as much as 10 percent. For intermediate and long-term investments, which offer the safer course for most moderate investors, basic values should be reexamined before deciding to sell at a loss. Does the stock have genuine potential for recovery? Is there a genuine tax reason for selling, or conversely, for postponing the sale for another tax year? Does the stock pay a large enough dividend to make waiting for recovery worthwhile?

When buying stocks, ignore all tips. Base your "buy" decisions on sound investment logic and yardsticks of value. Buy high-grade, recommended stocks and keep them until their full value seems to be achieved, at least for a reasonable future period. Avoid churning. Keep track of your broker's advice and remember that his chief function is to buy and sell stock, not to be an investment analyst.

You should not buy everything at its low nor switch out of the market at its high. One proverb that distills Wall Street's wisdom says: "Bulls make money; bears make money; pigs never make money."

CHAPTER 5

Choosing a Broker

A careful investor will always try to learn as much as possible about securities. He will not rely entirely on a broker's recommendations. Even so, the help of a good broker can be a major factor in successful investing.

There are a number of technical guidelines to be considered when choosing a broker. However, in the end, the success of your decision depends in large part on the achievement of a useful personal relationship. Investing and risking your money is a highly personal affair. Thus, finding a broker in whom you can have confidence is most important.

You can obtain the names of brokerage houses which are members of major stock exchanges from your banker, lawyer, your employer's pension and welfare fund administrators, from friends who are in the market, or even from the telephone book. You then can visit various brokers' offices and discuss your investment objectives. The office manager will recommend the registered representative he feels will be best suited to you.

Your choice of a broker may be limited by the amount of money you are prepared to invest in stocks. Many brokers hesitate to accept accounts with less than $10,000 to invest. In fact, the problem of serving the small investor has been the subject of much soul-searching in the investment industry in recent years. Some brokers simply refuse small investors; others keep their accounts dormant by refusing to compensate salesmen on transactions that generate very small commissions. It costs as much to put a small trade through the machinery of a broker's office as it does a large one. For a time, a $15 surcharge on each transaction was in effect to minimize losses on very small accounts.

There has been some discussion on Wall Street of trying to separate the customer who requires continuing service from the one who only wants the broker to execute an occasional order. Special charges for custodial accounts, in which the broker holds the customer's securities and transmits dividends, have been proposed, as have charges for research services.

Merrill Lynch, Pierce, Fenner & Smith, the nation's largest brokerage house, recently moved about 50,000 of its smaller accounts into twenty-three branch offices around the country. One representative handles the 2,000 or more accounts in each office. The customer receives a monthly statement, Merrill Lynch's quarterly review of the market, and recommendations of specific stocks.

Another major brokerage company proposed that statements of account be sent quarterly instead of monthly except when the customer expressly asks for a monthly statement or when there have been transactions in his account.

While the small investor may lack weight on Wall Street, his numbers make him a major public relations concern of the Big Board and the Securities and Exchange Commission. Soon after the surcharge on commissions was imposed in 1970, the New York Stock Exchange created an Investors' Service Bureau, an expansion of the Conduct Committee to which an investor who felt he had been wronged by a member could complain. The Service Bureau took on the added task of helping the investor who couldn't get a broker to pay him any attention.

As far as access to the formal machinery of the exchange is concerned—that is, to buy or sell a stock—the great Wall Street houses have always been accessible to anyone. The smaller houses, understandably, and especially in hard times, feel that they cannot afford the drain of little accounts that do not pay their way.

The catch to the Big Board's efforts is that what the small investor needs is not merely formal service. At any well-run brokerage, the salesmen are as courteous to the $1,000, twice-a-year customer as they are to an in-and-outer whose business reaches $10,000 a year. What the little fellow does not command is the assiduous keeping-in-touch reserved for the man who helps the salesman meet his quota. As long as stock brokerage is a commission business, it is unlikely that he will.

An investor who expects to trade actively will do well to ask how many accounts are handled by the man in charge of his account. This person is variously called the customer's man, registered representative, or salesman. Some salesmen can competently handle 200 or 300 accounts, but it is important to know that your man can give you the time and service you require.

"Registered representative" is the exact title of the salesman or customer's man. He becomes one by passing a test administered by the New York Stock Exchange. He must know the rules of the major exchanges as well as of the Securities and Exchange Commission and have a rudimentary knowledge of security analysis.

When choosing a broker, you should have definite objectives in mind. For example, are you willing to put your money in a discretionary account, which allows the broker to buy and sell at will? In the hands of competent and ethical brokers, this type of account may pay off, sometimes spectacularly. However, it has been the road to financial disaster for many an unwary investor whose broker was less than astute or even unscrupulous.

Most investors who are fairly knowledgeable about investment problems prefer *not* to let their stockbrokers decide when and what to buy. Furthermore, most brokers will decline this responsibility. Some investors want the broker to call them frequently with buy and sell recommendations and investment ideas. Others are put off by hard selling, preferring to evaluate their stocks less often.

A number of investors choose to go it alone. They use a broker primarily to execute their buy and sell decisions and to take advantage of the

Stockbroker discusses market fluctuations with a client.

investment research services offered by most brokerage firms. Research analysis is available in great quantity from the large multi-branch wire houses. These firms maintain extensive research departments to publish market letters, to provide individual company analysis, and to make buy-sell recommendations.

The analysis offered by brokerage houses varies greatly in quality and thus should be used with caution. Moreover, small investors do not always receive research bulletins in time to take advantage of a price movement. Before a study reaches the general run of clients, its contents often are leaked to the banks, pension plans, mutual funds and other institutional investors which today dominate stock market trading. Furthermore, more than half of most firms' investment advice goes out over the telephone, and customers' men naturally tend to favor their best clients in determining the sequence of their calls.

Although a brokerage research report may not contain new or significant information, the opinion expressed by a report which is circulated to thousands of clients and often quoted by newspapers can affect the price of the stock discussed. The investor should be wary of making a belated purchase of stock marked up by publicity.

Prompt execution of trading orders is important to the active investor and may be a consideration in his decision to deal with a large or small firm. Stock exchange officials tend to dismiss suggestions that any one member firm, large or small, can execute orders faster than any other. However, some large houses maintain as, many as seventeen floor men to speed the placing of orders at exchange trading posts. This sometimes gives their customers an edge over investors whose brokerage firms maintain smaller staffs. When a sudden news development prompts investors all over the country to ask their brokers to buy a stock, orders placed first may be executed at lower prices than later orders.

In general, the large houses exercise more rigid controls over their customers' men. For instance, some brokers are restricted to recommending issues selected by the firm's research department unless they obtain approval from their supervisor. While this precaution serves to protect the investor from fashionable tips which may be unwise, it also can cause him to miss fast-breaking investment opportunities that will not wait for the slow-moving head office process required to obtain the "recommended" stamp.

How to Work With Your Broker

After learning all you can about the background and experience of the individual assigned to your account, you should analyze your investment objectives and discuss them with the broker. Usually he will ask you whether you want stocks that will provide immediate high income, medium-term capital gains, long-term growth, or conservation of capital.

You can tell a great deal about a broker by discussing the investments he recommends to meet your special goals and requirements. Try to see if he really knows the stocks and whether he has a general awareness of business conditions. A careful representative will not offer tips or rumors; he will list facts on earnings, prospects and similar data to support his recommendations. In fact, he may not make firm recommendations at all, preferring instead to suggest a number of possible stocks that suit your investment objectives.

When asking the broker for advice on the selection of securities, the investor should never lose sight of the broker's objective, which is to earn a living on commissions from the purchase and sale of stocks. The prudent investor does not invest a substantial amount all at once. He places a few small orders to see how well they are executed and how his association with the broker is working out.

A good broker should be able to provide his client with the following information on any stock either at the time of the request or by the next day:

• The stock's current-year estimated earnings; estimated earnings for next year; earnings for the past five years.

• The high and low market price for the year.

• A copy of the Standard & Poor's or other data sheet on the stock in question.

• Information on any important development in the stock owned by the client.

• Documentation for his recommendations on the purchase or sale of stock using "hard" facts from the firm's research department.

Before starting an account with a new broker, you may want to find out his "track record" on recommendations. One way to do this is to have him introduce you to another of his clients. You might also ask for samples of the last dozen reports compiled by the broker's research department. This prevents the broker from selecting only the best reports.

Some investors, seeking to divorce the selection of securities from the stock brokerage function, turn to bank trust departments, which provide investment handling services of various types. These range from supervised investing, including buy-and-sell recommendations, to non-supervised accounts that provide only custodial and income-collection services.

Bank Trust Services

The First National City Bank of New York, for example, offers an Investment Selection Service for accounts of $25,000 or more. The bank charges a fee of 1 percent of the market value of the securities in the account. The minimum annual fee is $250. The bank will accept accounts with less than $25,000 if the investor considers the services attractive at the minimum fee. Under this plan the investor still pays brokerage commissions on trades made for his account, but the paperwork is simplified. In addition, the investor receives the services of the bank's research and economics departments. The management fee is tax deductible in almost all cases.

If you prefer not to do the research required for investments, bank services may be useful. You also can obtain professional management by investing in mutual funds or by consulting investment counselors and managers who perform such services. Although most will accept only substantial accounts, some accept accounts containing as little as $5,000. One such firm notes that its fee is partially balanced by combining clients' transactions in round lots. This saves on commissions.

Many of the services provided by trust departments can be obtained from a broker without the additional fee if you allow him to keep your stocks in his firm's name (called the street name). In the case of active accounts with as many as five or six transactions a year, brokers prefer to hold the stock certificates instead of sending them back and forth by registered mail. The broker will accumulate dividends in your account, send them to you as designated—monthly, for example—and give you a monthly statement of your account. You can help your broker, incidentally, by not calling him about matters such as late dividends during market trading hours when he is busy with transactions.

Some investors, fearing loss if the firm goes bankrupt, are reluctant to leave securities in the broker's name. However, the small investor received some safeguard against loss in 1970 when Congress approved the Securities Investor Protection Corporation. The SIPC now provides up to $50,000 in insurance, including $20,000 in cash, in much the same way that bank savings accounts are guaranteed by the Federal Deposit Insurance Corporation.

On the other hand, there are certain advantages in holding your own securities. You receive company reports a little sooner, and you can use the stocks as collateral for loans. If you do hold your own stock certificates, keep them in a safe place, preferably a safe deposit box. Never sign a certificate until you are ready to dispose of it and always use registered mail for sending securities. A lost or stolen certificate that has not been signed can be replaced, although at some inconvenience and expense, namely an affidavit and a surety bond which costs about 4 percent of the current market value of the stock.

Even if you do not leave your securities with a broker, you still may want to reassure yourself of the broker's stability. It is worth studying brokers' financial statements to determine whether they have adequate capital and whether a high proportion of assets are in cash and safe securities such as government and municipal bonds or in less dependable assets such as exchange memberships, office equipment, and leasehold improvements. Note also the amount of cash listed in the broker's assets compared to the value of securities. A small amount of cash and a large sum in securities owned by the brokerage firm may be risky since the value of securities can shrink.

CHAPTER 6

Financial Analysts: The Men Who Select Your Stocks

For the investor, the most significant individual in the securities industry may well be the person who selects the stocks recommended for purchase or sale. In general, small investors are guided by stock salesmen. In firms with research departments, however, the actual selection of securities is made by a financial analyst who passes the recommendations on to the salesman. There are also independent investment counselors who will perform this service for a fee.

Financial analysts are employed in all segments of the financial industry including commercial banking, brokerage and investment banking, insurance, investment counseling, mutual funds, endowment and pension funds, and financial publishing. A financial analyst may study the securities of specific companies, or he may specialize in one or more industries. This requires a thorough knowledge not only of the companies and industries concerned, but also of their relative competitive positions and the underlying economic conditions that affect their profitability.

A financial analyst attempts to keep abreast of the corporate product-research and marketing programs, the plant expansion plans, and the accounting and labor policies of the companies or industries in which he specializes. He also studies regulatory, political, and international developments.

Ideally, the analyst should also be a keen student of stock market action. Stock market movements depend upon opinion as much as upon fact. The successful trader often knows where the market is going before the analyst. The analyst knows *why* a given stock *should* move up or down; the trader senses *when* it *will* do so.

However, knowledge, said John Locke, cannot go beyond experience. When President Nixon announced the ninety-day wage-price freeze in August, 1971, he initiated a course with which the country was unfamiliar during peacetime. The first reaction of the stock market was an upsurge of prices. That was followed by general unease, as everyone pondered the implications of trying to harness the huge, volatile American economy. In October, 1971, one of Wall Street's major houses published a list of 134 stocks that might be bought for short-term appreciation. Within a month nearly a third of the stocks on the list had made new lows for the year.

The following year, as all the indicators of

national well-being pointed upward, the stock
market remained sullenly static until autumn.
Finally the conviction grew that we could work
very well within the framework of control established under Phase II. The very forces that had
held the market back began to push it forward.
The magic 1,000 mark of the Dow-Jones industrial average was attained almost exactly a year
after the trough of the post-freeze sag.

Perhaps the most important responsibility of
an analyst is to assess the quality of company
management. It is also the most difficult. One vet-
eran analyst expressed it this way:

> The automobile industry rarely has two good
> years in a row. That rhythm is accentuated in
> the tire industry because the cars of a poor
> year all wear out their tires in the next poor
> year, so the replacement and original equip-
> ment markets reinforce the cyclical swings.
> On the other hand, there is the steady growth
> of the whole market. Take it all together, and
> the chief executive officer of a tire company
> who comes in in the cyclical trough can look
> like a world-beater for a year or even two
> years. It takes four or five years to judge
> how much of a tire company's success is auto-
> matic and how much is owed to the c.e.o.
> (chief executive officer). By that time every-
> body else knows as much as you know.

A financial analyst obtains information from a
wide variety of sources. He visits plants and interviews corporation executives. He reads the financial press and periodicals as well as industry trade
journals. He seeks financial and other information
from stockholders reports, from reports filed with

the Securities and Exchange Commission, from the stock exchanges, from government and trade statistics, and from the various financial publishing companies.

He analyzes this information to estimate the potential future earnings of the companies he follows and to determine the valuation of these earnings by measures of relative quality and risk. He then translates this knowledge into probable market price objectives.

Some brokerage houses, especially smaller over-the-counter firms, do not employ financial analysts. Instead, research and advisory service is provided either by outside sources, such as Argus Research, Inc., which supplies research information to many stockbrokers, or by partners and salesmen who spend part of their time doing research.

Investment advisers who counsel others for a fee are required to register with the SEC under the Investment Advisers Act. Publishers of advisory services, periodic reports for subscribers, and market letters are included, as well as those who supervise portfolios for clients. However, only those who act principally as investment advisers are entitled to represent themselves as "investment counsel."

Investment Counselors

Investment counsel firms vary in size from one- or two-man concerns to large organizations with hundreds of employees. Usually they cater to the investor whose portfolio is of considerable value. In fact, many firms refuse to accept individuals who have less than $200,000 to invest.

Aside from the SEC, which acts in cases of out-and-out fraud or misrepresentation, the qualifica-

tion of investment counselors is the concern of
two industry groups: the Institute of Chartered
Financial Analysts and the Investment Counsel
Association of America. Both associations aim at
achieving professional recognition similar to that
of accountants. They hope eventually to require
higher standards for their calling. It is an uphill
endeavor, since these organizations lack the power
to prevent less qualified persons from engaging in
investment analysis or counseling without super-
vision.

On the other hand, the standards set by these
organizations can serve as guidelines for investors
who wish to retain independent investment counsel. Such counsel, the Investment Counsel Association recommends, should be based on "an approach
influenced solely by the objectives and needs of
the client. . . . Not by the advice of a broker's representative. Not recommendations of an underwriter. Not word from a securities dealer. Not a
trust department judgment and opinion. Not hot
news from a trusted friend. Not random information from a research bulletin or tip sheet."

Choosing an Investment Counselor

The decision to retain a particular investment
counselor should be followed by a personal meet-
ing to determine whether the investor and adviser
suit each other. Best results require full and frank
evaluation by each side. The more the counselor
knows about the client, the better he can advise
him. He should know the source and nature of
his client's present and future assets, income, family obligations and desires, investment philosophy,
and personal propensities.

In a typical investment counseling firm, an investor's account is assigned to an account supervisor. This is usually an experienced individual whose main task is the management of portfolios. It is his duty to select appropriate securities for the client after he and the client agree on the objectives of a portfolio plan.

In most firms, the account supervisor selects securities from a list based on recommendations from the firm's research department and approved by a committee which generally includes the heads of both the portfolio management department and the research department. He will follow portfolio holdings closely and recommend changes, keeping in touch by telephone, letter, and in person.

The client receives a full and detailed tabulation of the portfolio. For tax reasons and other considerations, it is not always practical or wise to buy or sell quickly. A portfolio program may take months or even years to complete.

The cash and securities comprising the portfolio are rarely in the possession of the investment counselor. The client, or his designated custodian, holds the securities, buying and selling as recommended by the counselor. Some investment counselors will not accept commissions on transactions conducted for their own or other non-client accounts which might conflict with their clients' interests.

Fees Charged

There is no apparent uniformity in the fees charged by investment counselors. Some negotiate fees on the basis of time spent on an account. Others have fixed-fee schedules geared to asset values. In general, fees run from $\frac{1}{2}$ to 2 percent a year of the asset value of the holdings being managed. The code of the Investment Counsel Association, which has fewer than 100 member firms, declares that compensation for investment management services should consist "exclusively of direct charges to clients for services rendered and should not be contingent on profits, upon the number or value of transactions executed, nor upon the maintenance of any minimum income."

Many brokerage firms offer special portfolio management services for a separate fee. Some offer this service without charge. Others derive their fees from the commission income realized on portfolio transactions either by an addition to the commission or by reducing the fee charged by the amount of the commission.

In general, professional money managers are not attracted to the investor whose holdings range between $10,000 and $100,000. Accounts of this size do not offer enough financial incentive. These investors usually invest on their own, rely on the advice of a broker, or seek professional management through a mutual fund.

Supermarket-Style Counselors   Another alternative exists, however. There are a growing number of investment counselors who specialize in handling small accounts. They rely on advertising in newspapers and financial magazines to attract enough clients to make small fees pay. Choosing an investment counselor, whatever the size of the holding involved, is a difficult task; almost anyone can set himself up in the business. Beyond the formality of registering with the SEC, no experience is required; no examinations are taken. There are nearly 4,000 registered investment advisers of widely-varying capability, ranging from moonlighting taxicab drivers to Harvard Business School Ph.D.'s.

Among the better known of the established investment counseling firms that handle small accounts are Danforth Associates of Wellesley, Massachusetts, and Spear and Staff of Boston, which manages total investments estimated at $30 to $60 million in asset value. Danforth accepts accounts containing as little as $5,000. One advantage of its service, it points out, is that its fees are balanced, at least in part, by the savings on commissions the firm can make by combining individual transactions in round lots.

The La Jolla, California, firm of Mansfield Mills, another representative investment counselor, handles accounts of $10,000 or more, charging a fee of 2 percent a year on the first $50,000 and 1 percent for accounts over that amount.

Many of the financial counselors who accept moderate investors restrict themselves to clients whose holdings total $10,000 or more. Generally these firm charge a fee of 2 percent a year on the first $50,000 and 1 percent for holdings over that amount. Thus, on a $10,000 account, the investment counselor's fee would be $200 in comparison to the $50 in management fees and expenses charged by a typical mutual fund for the management of a $10,000 holding. In addition to the $200 fee, the client pays the brokerage commissions on any transactions made in his behalf.

In a typical load mutual fund, the investor would pay a sales commission of $800 to $900 on a $10,000 purchase. Thus, the investment counsel plan is slightly less expensive than most mutual funds over a five-year period. On the other hand, the investment counsel arrangement entails greater expenses than for a no-load mutual fund.

Handling larger accounts is Wright Managed Investment Accounts of Bridgeport, Connecticut, whose fee is ½ percent of the market value of the account, with $750 per year minimum. Investment decisions are executed upon the recommendations of the well-known Wright Investor's Service. It reported a 15.8 percent compound annual rate for the ten-year period 1961-70, compared with a Dow-Jones industrial average of 6.3 percent, a New York Stock Exchange Composite of 7.2 percent, and a mutual fund index of 8.7 percent.

This period includes the three greatest stock market declines (1962, 1966, and 1969-70) in twenty-five years, as well as the 1963-65 and 1967-68 advances. From October 1, 1965 to December 31, 1970, Wright Managed Investment Accounts cited a comparative investment performance of 60 percent versus 10 percent for the Dow-Jones industrial average.

In a disclaimer customary in the financial industry, Wright emphasizes that "it should not be assumed that future results will be profitable or equal past performance." (Nor is the inclusion of the firms cited in this book intended to constitute an endorsement of any of them. They are cited only as prominent examples of this type of service.)

Perhaps the chief advantage offered by reputable "small account" money managers is a degree of flexibility not possible in mutual funds. The investment generally spreads over four to twelve stocks as compared with fifty or more in a mutual fund. This selectivity can result in superior gains. On the other hand, the risks are equally great.

There are also other advantages. The fee is tax

deductible. There is no temptation to churn accounts to earn brokerage commissions. The account can be handled to accommodate individual tax situations; profits can be taken to offset outside losses, or gains can be held to avoid tax liability.

A criticism sometimes made of the investment counselors who handle small accounts is that their recommendations tend to be standardized and that they cannot really give their clients much individual attention. If, say the critics, it were possible to make money on a $10,000 account without resorting to "supermarket" methods, the orthodox money managers would not turn them down.

An innovation in the investment counseling field —too recent for an informed judgment on how it will turn out—is what might be called the investment counseling clinic. A member of the National Association of Security Dealers, a mortgage broker, a bond dealer, a mutual fund salesman, and an insurance agent form an association and offer investment advice. In theory, at least, the adviser assigned to you will be just as happy to sell you an oil drilling participation or an annuity. The fact that commissions are pooled is supposed to rule out any conflict of interest between the investor and the adviser.

In general, what should the investor expect of his investment counselor? Most important, perhaps, are professional competence and the ability to minimize the impact of stock selections that have gone wrong and to maximize the gains afforded by good choices. It is relative achievement that counts. Using a baseball analogy cited by Charles D. Ellis in the *Financial Analysts Journal*, Babe Ruth set his historic record for home

runs in the same year that he established a record
for strike-outs. He is permanently enshrined for
the former instead of the latter because his successes greatly outweighed his defeats.

CHAPTER 7

The Corporate Report

A basic tool in the search for investment-quality stocks is the corporate annual report, which recapitulates the company's yearly performance for the benefit of the stockholders and offers clues to future strengths and weaknesses. Evaluation of a company's annual report requires experience, astuteness, and a talent for reading between the lines of the company president's letter to the stockholders.

Merrill Lynch's booklet *How to Read a Financial Report* gives this unusually candid view of how the prudent investor should approach the annual report:

All annual reports bring their readers written messages whose rhetoric ranges from murky to magnificently clear . . . The purpose of these messages is to put the best face possible on whatever has happened to the corporation during the year . . .

Most annual reports will delight you with exquisite pictures of plants and products, people and places . . . More and more annual reports are becoming lavish exercises in printing and publishing. This is fine so long as costs don't deprive stockholders of too much of their dividends.

So read the prose, enjoy the pictures, then turn to the balance sheet. You cannot miss it, for the balance sheet is the formidable section of numbers that somehow wind up all even. Its language may be thorny and its rows of figures seem as impenetrable as anything else in your annual report, but the balance sheet holds the key to your journey out of the jungle and into the cultivated country of facts.

Even in the "cultivated country of facts," however, there is still unknown terrain. The investor must remain wary of numerous pitfalls, especially those inherent in the accounting profession's methods of reporting corporate financial operations. Companies can brighten a drab balance sheet by making favorable assumptions. As long as the accountant faithfully records these assumptions in his notes, he feels that his duty to the reader of the report is fulfilled.

In recent years there has been increasing criticism of annual reports that are often less than candid. The investment industry and the accountants themselves are the main critics. Many complaints, according to a report by Wall Street Surveys (Robert S. Taplinger Associates), focus on the lack of precise, factual information and figures in such areas as production growth, market share, and industry trends. Other critics decry "attempts to obfuscate diluted capitalization" and object to insufficient breakdown of expenses.

A Federal Trade Commission study of corporate mergers released in 1970 cited the case of the Automatic Sprinkler Corporation of America. The study noted that Automatic Sprinkler, reporting a 100 percent rise in after-tax earnings from 1966 to 1967, did not include in the comparative 1966 figure the earnings of companies it acquired in 1967. Such a comparison would have shown a 15 percent decline in earnings.

Despite these caveats about annual reports, it should be emphasized that money managers and investment advisers put great emphasis on this area of analysis, particularly after being chastened by a bear market such as occurred in 1969-70. A 1971 study by Research & Forecasts, Inc., (Ruder & Finn) indicated that "In a bear market, finance becomes king." Interviews with 120 analysts from brokerage firms, banks, and investment advisory organizations revealed that professionals were *again* giving close scrutiny to annual reports, corporate balance sheets, and financial footnotes.

"During the late 1960s, many money managers and analysts, too, forgot there was such a thing as a balance sheet. They were interested only in growth without regard to how this growth would be financed," commented the chief investment officer of a fund group quoted in the study.

The experts also emphasize that financial reports are only half-valuable in a vacuum. To be truly useful they must be compared to the financial reports of competitors in the industry and to the reports of that firm from preceding years.

Emphasizing the importance of a company's competitive position in its industry, one money manager reported that he especially looks for data showing that a company is increasing its share of the market. This indicates that it not only is increasing its advantage over the competition, but also that it is obtaining a compounded gain as the economy grows.

No. 1 Fact: Earnings-Per-Share   Perhaps the single most significant statistic in the annual report is the earnings-per-share of common stock. But be sure to take a second look to see if any convertible bonds, warrants, and other convertible securities are outstanding. These can dilute the earnings-per-share if they are converted to common stock. More and more accountants have been insisting that annual statements tell what. the earnings would be if these securities were converted.

Thus you need to look for two figures: earnings-per-share and earnings-per-share "diluted." A large difference can affect the potential price-earnings ratio significantly. The P/E, which is the market price of a share divided by earnings-per-share, is the basic figure to be used in viewing the record of the stock over a period of years and in comparing the company's common stock to other similar stocks.

Differences in corporate accounting methods can also confuse the true picture of earnings. There is a broad field for deft balance sheet juggling in the allocations of expenditures between expenses and investment. Some companies capitalize more on such expenses as research and development or the start-up costs of new plants than do others. These choices affect reported earnings. One method is as legitimate as another as long as it is followed consistently. A danger signal flashes when a year-to-year change is made that gives a significantly better picture of earnings than the one that is being discarded.

The method of reporting income should be closely examined. In most well-established companies, there usually is no problem. Some land-development and franchising companies in the late 1960s counted as current income the promissory notes given them by lot buyers or franchises. As a result, incautious investors suffered serious losses. It was not until late in 1969 that accountants belatedly challenged this practice.

In addition to the fundamental facts about earnings-per-share and the trend of such earnings over the past five or ten years as listed in the annual report, investors also look for the following indicators of a company's financial position and future prospects:

Other Facts to Look For

Book Value

The net book value per share of common stock is the amount of assets attributable to each share if the company were liquidated and the bond-holders and preferred stockholders paid. Book value has little relation to market price. Conservative investment analysts hold, however, that a current market price of more than twice the book value may be a warning that the market price is out of line, unless the company has unusually good growth prospects.

On the other hand, stocks of old established companies that are no longer profitable may be quoted on the market for as low as 50 cents per dollar of stockholder's equity. This usually occurs when the company has property listed in its books at a cost far below its current value. Such hidden assets are one reason why older companies are sometimes targets of corporate raiders.

In addition to providing a frame of reference for the fair market price of common stock, as outlined above, John Winthrop Wright, an investment counselor, emphasizes two other reasons why "book value" is important to investors:

1—*To determine how profitable a company is.* The profit rate of any company can be found by dividing the net income by the book value. The result, expressed as a percentage, provides the company's profit rate of earnings on shareholders' equity capital. In recent years, the average company listed on the New York Stock Exchange had a profit rate (PR) of about 11 percent. Some of the most profitable firms have PR's of 20 or 30 percent. Since you can earn at least 5 percent on a savings account, and from 6 to 8 percent with high grade bonds, why buy stock in a company that has a PR of less than 10 percent? Generally speaking, the companies whose stocks sell at low price/earnings ratios have low PR's.

2—*To estimate the earned growth rate.* The only growth that has any real meaning to the investor is earned growth. This shows how fast your share of equity capital invested in the corporation is growing each year. The earned growth rate (EGR) is the annual rate at which retained earnings are reinvested in the company. Suppose a company has a book

Simplified Balance Sheet From a Corporate Report

ASSETS		Millions
Telephone Plant and Investments		
Telephone plant—in service and under construction		$75,922
Investments		3,663
	Total	79,585
Current Assets		
Cash		1,487
Receivables		3,917
Materials and supplies		544
Prepaid expenses		177
	Total	6,125
Deferred Charges		1,007
	TOTAL ASSETS	$86,717

LIABILITIES AND CAPITAL		
Equity		
Common shares		$17,332
Preferred shares		2,862
Minority interests in subsidiaries		899
Reinvested earnings		16,126
	Total	37,219
Debt		
Long-term		32,524
Interim (due in year but to be refinanced)		2,471
	Total	34,995
Current Liabilities		
Accounts payable		2,200
Accrued taxes		1,136
Advance billings, customers' deposits		773
Dividends payable		647
Accrued interest		632
	Total	5,388
Deferred Credits		
Accumulated deferred income taxes		6,210
Unamortized investment in tax credits		2,730
Other		175
	Total	9,115
	TOTAL LIABILITIES AND CAPITAL	$86,717

Source: Consolidated Balance Sheet, American Telephone & Telegraph Company, December 31, 1976, Annual Report

value of $10 per share, earns $1 per share, and pays 60 cents a share in dividends. This leaves 40 cents for reinvestment. The new book value would be $10.40, and the EGR would be 4 percent. Remember, EGR concerns only that portion of the increase resulting from operating profits, not from the sale of more stock or property or from the purchase of another firm.

Current Ratio

This is an important yardstick that enables you to judge whether a company has a sound working capital position. Using this ratio, you can estimate how liquid the company is. To find the current ratio, divide current assets by current liabilities. Usually a high ratio means the business is in good condition. This varies by industry, however. A utility, for instance, can safely operate with a lower current ratio, say one-to-one, than a firm in the highly competitive garment industry. A two-to-one ratio of current assets over current liabilities is considered adequate for most industries. Such a ratio, however, does not reveal whether the current assets, even if high, are being used to best advantage or whether receivables and inventory are too high for maximum profitability. This is a consideration to watch for and, if possible, to check through further research.

Capital Structure

Note how much of a company's capital is derived from common stock and how much from bonds and preferred stock, both of which have prior claims to earnings. A normal capital structure for an industrial company would be 50 percent from common stocks, 25 percent from bonds, and 25 percent from preferred stock. The company with lower common stock capitalization may be subject to wide fluctuations in overall earnings-per-share.

Ratio of Debt to Equity or Worth

This figure measures the amount of debt in comparison to assets. Usually a ratio of two dollars in assets for every one dollar of debts is considered fair except in the case of public utilities, which have a high debt and thus a lower ratio. A high ratio may be a sign of safety since there are considerable assets to cushion both stockholders and creditors. However, a ratio that is much higher than usual could indicate that the company is holding onto too much cash instead of using it to increase profits.

Net Profit Ratio

This figure indicates a company's efficiency. To obtain the net profit ratio, divide total net profit by total net sales. It should be compared with figures for previous years, with other companies in the same industry, and with other industries.

Profit to Net Worth

Divide the earnings by the net worth to obtain the company's yield or return on its total investment.

Internal vs. External Growth

Look for evidence in the report and in the accompanying president's letter that shows whether increases in total earnings and sales volume are generated by internal growth or through acquisitions. Increases through internal growth are a sign of effective management in a dynamic industry or market.

Turnover

This can be determined by obtaining the ratio of sales to accounts receivable. This figure can have important consequences in periods of tight money. During such times, slow paying accounts may force the company into very expensive short-term money markets, thereby depressing earnings substantially.

Retained Earnings

This figure indicates the amount of net profits being held by the company and the amount being paid out to stockholders. Many companies nowadays pay out less than 50 percent. Growth companies, so called because they plow back much of their earnings, may pay out only 20 to 30 percent. A high payout provides immediate income. Investors hoping for future growth will accept low payouts now for the sake of capital gains in the future.

The five- or ten-year summary of results found in an annual report should be studied to determine these trends:

• The trend and consistency of sales fluctuations.
• The trend of earnings, particularly in relation to sales and the economy.
• The trend of net earnings as a percentage of sales.
• Net earnings-per-share of common stock.
• Dividends and dividend policy.

When reading an annual report, the investor should look for special treatment of items such as tax write-offs, leases, pension plans, stock options, mergers, application of funds from foreign and domestic subsidiaries, and bank loans. A large outstanding bank loan, for instance, may be tied to an agreement that restricts the payment of dividends until the loan is satisfied. Often, although there is growing criticism of this practice, such pertinent information is restricted to the fine print of auditors' footnotes.

Watch the Footnotes

Some examples of important subjects that are often covered in footnotes are these:

• Changes in the firm's method of depreciating fixed assets.

• Changes in the value of stock outstanding due to stock dividends and splits.

• Details of stock options granted to officers and employees.

• Employment contracts, profit-sharing, pension, and retirement plans.

• Contingent liabilities representing claims or lawsuits pending.

A shareholder also should take note of the following specific events that may be listed in the annual report or in other company communications:

• Announcement of a joint venture, merger, or acquisition.

• The acquisition or loss of a significant contract.

• A significant new product or discovery.

• A call of securities for redemption.

• The borrowing of a significant amount of funds.

- The public or private sale of significant amounts of additional securities.
- The company's involvement in significant litigation.
- The purchase or sale of a major asset.
- A major change in the company's capital investment plans.
- A significant labor dispute or disputes with important subcontractors or suppliers.
- The establishment of a program to make purchases of the company's own shares.
- An offer for the company to purchase another company's securities.

The President's Letter   One of the more important sections of the annual report, according to many investment analysts, is the president's letter. One analyst has commented: "I always try to read between the lines to see if management is saying something important without really spelling it out . . . For example, if I know a labor contract is coming up and the letter doesn't say anything about it, I get suspicious. . ."

The president's letter also may indicate what he is trying to do with the company and how effectively various divisions of the company are contributing to company profits.

The SEC mandated a number of changes to make annual reports more informative, beginning in 1974. One of these is a breakdown into lines of a multiline company's activities. The shareholder can make up his mind whether he approves a prestige line that does not pay its way, and see whether an acquisition that was highly touted is really all that valuable.

Perhaps more vital is that little box informing the shareholder that he may have on request a copy of the company's latest 10-K report. The 10-K report, filed with the SEC each time a company sells stock, borrows money, or elects directors, spells out every detail of the company's business so that no one can say in court that he was deceived and wants his money back or some action rescinded. Lawyer-fashion, it leans over backward to tell all.

Some 300 common and preferred stocks are traded at posts on this New York
Stock Exchange trading floor.

Marketplace: The Exchanges

Although trading in securities takes place mostly in New York, there are also three principal regional exchanges: Midwest in Chicago, Pacific Coast in San Francisco and Los Angeles, and Philadelphia-Baltimore-Washington. Smaller registered exchanges are in Boston, Cincinnati, Detroit, Salt Lake City, and Spokane. Those in the west concentrate on low-priced mining stocks. Three small exempt exchanges, so-called because they do not have to register with the Securities and Exchange Commission, operate in Colorado Springs, Honolulu, and Richmond.

The New York Stock Exchange (NYSE), the American Stock Exchange (AMEX), also in New York, the Midwest Exchange, and the Pacific

Coast Exchange account for 98 percent of the dollar volume and 97 percent of the shares traded on all exchanges. The New York Stock Exchange was established in 1792 and today is the nation's major exchange. It lists over 1,800 stocks comprising the securities of the country's major companies. The larger regional exchanges list about 500 companies each, mostly regional and local concerns, while the smaller exchanges each list around 100 companies. They also do extensive trading in shares listed on the New York exchanges. About a third of the firms in the Pacific Coast Exchange are also members of the NYSE, and over 90 percent of the stocks it trades are listed on the New York exchanges. This holds true in lesser part for the Midwest Exchange. Because of the three-hour time differential, the Pacific Coast Exchange provides trading facilities after the close of the NYSE and AMEX.

To list its stock for trading on a securities exchange, a company must give detailed information about its operations to the SEC and to the exchange itself. The various exchanges have different standards for listing; the most rigid is that of the NYSE. To qualify for an original listing, a company must have a minimum of one million shares outstanding. It must have at least 2,000 shareholders, at least 1,700 of whom must own 100 shares or more apiece. The publicly held shares should have a minimum sales value of $16 million. In addition, the company must have earned $2.5 million in the latest year for which it has reported and at least $2 million during each of five preceding years.

The NYSE is a private association with 1,366 members. Each has purchased a seat, or membership, on the exchange. The exchange's trading floor in its building on Broad Street has twenty-two trading posts. These are manned by exchange members called specialists, who buy and sell one or more of the 1,800 securities listed on the exchange.

The specialist is expected to use his own funds to buy stocks offered for sale when there is no public buyer for the stock and to sell shares from his own account when no member of the public is willing to sell shares sought by a would-be buyer. He also keeps the book in the stocks in which he specializes. This means that he acts for other brokers who cannot wait at one post until the prices specified by their customers' buy and sell orders are reached. When a specialist executes an order for another broker's customer, he receives part of that broker's commission on the order. Specialists derive much of their earnings from these commissions.

About one-fourth of the NYSE's members are specialists. Perhaps half of the members are partners or officers of "commission houses," brokerage firms that execute customers' orders to buy and sell. Some members, known as floor brokers, execute orders for the commission brokers or for outsiders such as over-the-counter houses, banks, and other institutions. The floor broker, who has no customers of his own, is also called the two-dollar broker because many years ago he received that amount as his commission on each 100-share lot.

Until mid-1975, a single house survived of several that once specialized in odd-lot trading—buying or selling fewer than 100 shares at a price a fraction above or below the last recorded 100-share transaction. Now that function has been taken over by the NYSE directly for its listed shares, and Merrill Lynch offers odd-lot trades at the same price as the last round-lot trade.

On the New York Exchange a customer's order is handled as follows: Suppose Jane Baxter of New York decides to buy 100 shares of the American Telephone and Telegraph Company. She asks her broker for a "quote" on the price of AT&T shares. He punches the code "T" for AT&T on the firm's push-button Quotron device, which is linked to the NYSE data computer. Almost instantaneously, the computer flashes back the following printout on a small desk television in the broker's office: "AT&T last sale 49¼—offered 49¼—bid 49 (+)." The plus sign is an "up tick," meaning the last sale was made in a rising market for the shares.

The registered representative tells Mrs. Baxter that 100 AT&T shares will cost her approximately $4,925, plus a commission of $68. This includes a $15 maximum surcharge imposed on transactions of 1,000 shares or less since April, 1970. Mrs. Baxter decides to buy, and the broker draws up an order for the purchase of 100 shares of AT&T "at the market." The order is teletyped to the exchange floor and relayed to the firm's broker nearest to Post 15 where "T" is traded and where all bids and offers must take place.

Meanwhile, a Chicago man, James Jones, decides he wants to sell 100 shares of AT&T. He calls his brokerage house, gets a "quote," and decides to sell. His order is wired or telephoned to the floor. Now both the Baxter broker and the Jones broker work their way into the AT&T "crowd" at Post 15. The Baxter broker calls out, "How's Telephone?" Someone—often as not, the specialist—calls the answer, "49 to a quarter."

At this point, the Baxter broker could buy the 100 shares offered at 49 and the Jones broker could sell his 100 at 49. On the other hand, each must try to get the best price for his customer. The Baxter broker notes that he cannot buy 100 shares at 49 since someone previously bid that price and found no sellers. He also knows that no one thus far has offered to buy at the requested price of $49\frac{1}{4}$. This is noted by the Jones broker also. Logically, it occurs to both brokers to try to split the difference. Thus, when the Baxter broker calls out a bid of $49\frac{1}{8}$, the Jones broker shouts, "Sold at $49\frac{1}{8}$."

Each reports the completed transaction to his floor clerk so the customer can be notified. Meanwhile, an exchange clerk notes the transaction on an IBM card and puts the card into the optical scanner at the post. From there it is transmitted to the exchange central computer and to the ticker. In a few seconds, it appears automatically as "T. $49\frac{1}{8}$" on thousands of tickers in this country, Canada, and abroad.

Now Mrs. Baxter must pay for the shares she has purchased, and Mr. Jones must deliver the certificate shares he has sold. In the absence of any agreement to the contrary, this must be done by noon of the fifth business day following the day of the transaction. Saturdays, Sundays, and holidays are not counted. As the seller, Mr. Jones pays the New York State transfer tax, which ranges from $1\frac{1}{4}$ to 5 cents a share depending on the selling price of the stock. Since Mr. Jones is a non-resident, he pays 4 cents a share on stocks selling for $20 or more.

Ten-Year Performance of
300 Individual Stocks
January 1, 1967—January 1, 1977

	Percentage Gain or Loss		*Percentage Gain or Loss*
Addressograph-Multigraph	− 73	Bendix Corp.	+ 72
Air Products & Chemicals	+ 162	Bethlehem Steel	+ 37
Alabama Gas	− 47	Black & Decker Mfg.	+ 162
Alcoa	+ 10	Boeing	− 32
Alcon Laboratories	+ 475	Borg-Warner	+ 62
Allegheny Ludlum Steel	− 33	Bristol-Myers	+ 24
AMAX Corp.	+ 112	Brunswick Corp.	+ 141
American Brands	+ 48	Bucyrus-Erie	+ 376
American Can	− 17	Burroughs Corp.	+ 318
American Cyanamid	− 9	Campbell Soup	+ 45
American Home Products	+ 140	Cannon Mills	− 81
American Natural Resources	+ 15	Carborundum Co.	+ 60
American Standard	+ 53	Carnation Co.	+ 271
American Tel. & Tel.	+ 15	Carrier Corp.	+ 55
AMF, Inc.	+ 55	Carter-Wallace	− 42
AMP, Inc.	+ 191	Caterpillar Tractor	+ 75
Ampex	− 65	Celanese Corp.	+ 4
Amstar	+ 97	Central & South West	− 28
Anderson, Clayton	+ 257	Central Illinois Public Service	− 32
Anheuser-Busch	+ 55	Central Maine Power	− 13
Apeco	− 68	Chase Manhattan	− 27
Archer-Daniels-Midland	+ 675	Chemetron Corp.	− 16
Armco Steel	+ 38	Chesebrough-Ponds	+ 75
Ashland Oil	+ 6	Chicago Pneumatic Tool	+ 1
Atlantic Richfield	+ 167	Chrysler Corp.	− 34
Atlas Corp.	+ 48	Cincinnati Gas & Electric	− 15
Avco Corp.	− 39	CIT Financial	+ 39
Avon Products	+ 22	Cities Service	+ 24
Babcock & Wilcox	− 5	Cleveland Electric Illum.	− 16
Baker Industries	+ 99	Cluett, Peabody	− 48
BankAmerica	+ 162	Colgate-Palmolive	+ 196
Baxter Laboratories	+ 293	Columbia Gas System	+ 19
Beatrice Foods	+ 123	Combustion Engineering	+ 112
Beckman Instruments	+ 22	Cone Mills	+ 149
Beech Aircraft	+ 96	Consolidated Natural Gas	+ 28

	Percentage Gain or Loss			Percentage Gain or Loss
Continental Group	+ 20	Gamble-Skogmo	+ 5
Copperweld Steel	+ 72	Gardner-Denver	+ 88
Corning Glass Works	− 42	GATX Corp.	+ 1
Crane Co.	+ 290	General Electric	+ 26
Crown Zellerbach	+ 52	General Foods	− 16
Curtiss-Wright	+ 23	General Mills	+ 129
Dana Corp.	+ 243	General Motors	+ 19
Dan River	− 53	General Refractories	− 42
Deere & Co.	+ 86	General Telephone &	
Delta Airlines	− 2	Electronics	− 30
Detroit Edison	− 54	General Tire & Rubber	− 9
Diamond Shamrock	+ 117	Georgia-Pacific	+ 284
Disney (Walt) Productions	+ 533	Gerber Products	+ 3
Dome Mines	+ 208	Goodyear Tire & Rubber	+ 16
Dow Chemical	+ 323	Grace (W.R.) & Co.	− 41
Dresser Industries	+ 188	Grand Union	− 14
du Pont (E. I.) de Nemours	− 6	Greyhound Corp.	− 6
Duquesne Light Co.	− 34	Grolier, Inc.	− 94
Eastern Air Lines	− 78	Gulf Oil Corp.	− 2
Eastern Gas & Fuel	+ 398	Halliburton Co.	+ 862
Eastman Kodak	+ 35	Hammond Corp.	− 61
El Paso Natural Gas	− 17	Hanover Insurance	− 10
Emerson Electric	+ 130	Heinz (H.J.) Co.	+ 235
Emery Air Freight	+ 64	Heller International	+ 134
Engelhard Minerals & Chem.	+ 198	Hercules, Inc.	+ 28
Enserch Corp.	+ 53	Hershey Foods Corp.	− 8
Equitable Gas Co.	+ 10	Hewlett-Packard	+ 240
Esmark, Inc.	+ 101	Holly Sugar	+ 70
Ex-Cell-O Corp.	+ 16	Homestake Mining	+ 80
Exxon Corp.	+ 70	Household Finance	+ 8
Fairmont Foods	0	IBM	+ 92
Federal-Mogul Corp.	− 19	Idaho Power Co.	− 11
Federal Paper Board	+ 29	Ideal Basic Industries	+ 58
Ferro Corp.	+ 148	Ingersoll-Rand	+ 98
Firestone Tire & Rubber	+ 3	Inland Steel	+ 62
First Charter Financial	+ 222	Interco, Inc.	+ 163
Flintkote Co.	+ 33	Interlake, Inc.	+ 44
Florida Power & Light	− 25	International Flavors &	
FMC Corp.	− 18	Fragrances	+ 135
Ford Motor Co.	+ 59	International Harvester	− 12
Fruehauf Corp.	+ 11	International Minerals	− 9

	Percentage Gain or Loss			Percentage Gain or Loss
International Paper	+ 170		Monarch Machine Tool	+ 72
International Tel. & Tel.	− 7		Monsanto Co.	+ 118
Jewel Companies	+ 35		Montana Power Co.	− 13
Johns-Manville	+ 39		Murphy (G.C.) Co.	− 1
Johnson & Johnson	+ 311		Nabisco	+ 7
Joy Manufacturing	+ 280		Nalco Chemical	+ 126
Kaiser Aluminum & Chemical	− 13		National Distillers	+ 26
Kellogg Co.	+ 203		National Fuel Gas	0
Kerr-McGee	+ 153		National Gypsum	+ 18
Kimberly-Clark	+ 83		National Steel	+ 12
Koppers Co.	+ 287		National Tea	− 71
Kraftco Corp.	+ 37		NCR Corp.	+ 11
Kresge (S.S.)	+ 871		New England Electric Sys.	− 16
Laclede Gas	− 4		Newmont Mining	+ 54
Lehigh Portland Cement	+ 86		N.Y. State Electric & Gas	− 29
Libbey-Owens-Ford	− 6		NL Industries	− 25
Liggett & Myers	+ 3		Norfolk & Western	− 3
Lincoln National Corp.	+ 21		North American Coal	+ 253
Lockheed Aircraft	− 86		Northern Natural Gas	+ 97
Loews Corp.	+ 930		Northern States Power	− 12
Lone Star Industries	+ 53		Oklahoma Gas & Electric	− 32
Louisville Gas & Electric	− 16		Oklahoma Natural Gas	+ 82
Lowenstein (M) & Sons	− 1		Olin Corp.	+ 8
Lukens Steel	− 18		Outboard Marine	+ 67
Macy (R.H.) & Co.	+ 64		Owens-Corning Fiberglass	+ 102
Maremont Corp.	+ 61		Owens-Illinois, Inc.	+ 4
Marine Midland Banks	− 63		Pacific Tel. & Tel.	+ 20
Marshall Field & Co.	+1058		Panhandle Eastern Pipeline	+ 37
Martin Marietta	+ 22		Penn-Dixie Industries	− 42
Masco Corp.	+ 12		Pennwalt Corp.	− 26
Masonite Corp.	+ 216		Peoples Gas Co.	+ 40
May Department Stores	+ 47		Pepsico	+ 122
McGraw-Edison	− 4		Perkin-Elmer	+ 240
Mead Corp.	+ 41		Pfizer, Inc.	+ 26
Merck & Co.	+ 78		Phelps Dodge Corp.	+ 24
Mesta Machine	− 7		Philip Morris	+ 624
Middle South Utilities	− 34		Phillips Petroleum	+ 167
Minnesota Mining & Mfg.	+ 45		Pitney-Bowes	− 35
Mississippi River Corp.	+ 168		Pittston Co.	+ 782
Mobil Oil Corp.	+ 41		Polaroid	− 51
Molybdenum Corp.	− 32		PPG Industries	+ 113

	Percentage Gain or Loss			Percentage Gain or Loss
Procter & Gamble	+ 157		Southwestern Public Service	— 10
Public Service Electric & Gas	— 36		Sperry Rand	+ 43
Puget Sound Power & Light	+ 3		Square D Co.	+ 45
Quaker Oats	+ 114		Standard Brands	+ 75
Ralston Purina	+ 128		Standard Oil (Indiana)	+ 147
Rapid American Corp.	— 54		Standard Packaging	+ 11
Raybestos-Manhattan	— 31		Stauffer Chemical	+ 161
Raytheon	+ 129		Stewart-Warner	+ 38
RCA Corp.	— 25		Sunbeam Corp.	— 24
Republic Steel	— 16		Superior Oil	+ 90
Revere Copper & Brass	— 61		Tandy Corp.	+2165
Reynolds (R.J.) Industries	+ 98		Texas Gas Transmission	+ 76
Reynolds Metals	— 20		Texas Instruments	+ 106
Rio Grande Industries	+ 87		Texas Utilities	— 24
Robertshaw Controls	+ 95		Thiokol Chemical	+ 11
Royal Dutch Petroleum	+ 118		Timken Co.	+ 56
Safeway Stores	+ 109		Trans World Airlines	— 85
St. Joe Minerals	+ 123		Tri-Continental Corp.	— 4
St. Regis Paper	+ 123		Twentieth Century Fox	— 39
Santa Fe Industries	+ 41		Union Pacific Railroad	+ 173
Schering-Plough	+ 224		Uniroyal, Inc.	— 51
Schlumberger, Ltd.	+2327		United Merchants & Mfrs.	— 50
Scott Paper	— 24		U.S. Fidelity & Guaranty	+ 74
Sears, Roebuck	+ 54		U.S. Gypsum	— 6
Shell Oil	+ 31		Upjohn Co.	+ 13
Sherwin-Williams	— 11		Utah Power & Light	+ 32
Simmons Co.	+ 52		Western Union	— 45
Smith (A.O.) Corp	+ 57		Weyerhaeuser Co.	+ 444
SmithKline Corp.	+ 54		Williams Cos.	+ 84
Southern California Edison	— 41		Winn-Dixie Stores	+ 120
Southern Co.	— 43		Wisconsin Electric Power	+ 10
Southern Natural Gas	+ 65		Wrigley (Wm.), Jr.	+ 29
Southern Pacific Co.	+ 28		Xerox	— 11
Southern Railway	+ 193		Zenith Radio	— 41

**Types of
Orders**   Most stock market transactions take place at
the market. The buyer or seller authorizes the
broker to execute the order at the best price prevailing when the order reaches the exchange floor.
Some investors, however, use the limit order,
which enables them to specify the price at which
they wish to sell. The broker notes this instruction
and passes the limit order on to the specialist, who
enters it in his book. When and if the market
reaches the specified price—there is no guarantee
that it will do so—the order is executed and the
customer billed.

When the investor places a limit order, he tells
his broker whether it is to be effective for a day,
a week, a month, or until it is cancelled. A good-
till-cancelled order stands until it is executed, unless the investor withdraws it.

Another device used to insure that a stock is
sold at or around a stipulated price is the stop
order. This is triggered when the price of the
stock passes a certain point. The stop order then
becomes a market order.

Stop orders are widely used to stop a possible
loss or to protect a paper profit. Let's assume that
Mr. Jones bought AT&T at 50 in 1960 and saw
it rise to 70 in 1965. Then he grew uneasy about
the company's prospects and gave his broker a
stop loss order to sell if the price receded to 65.
That order is activated when the stock touches 65;
if the best price Mr. Jones's broker can get at the
next sale is 64¾, he must take it.

A similar order may be given by a short seller.
He sells stock he does not own in the expectation
of being able to buy it back at a lower figure. For
instance, he might sell a volatile stock like Chrys-
ler at 35, hoping to buy it again at 25. However,

to insure himself against a sharp rise in price, he orders the stock bought if it reaches 40. If the stock rises to that price, the buy stop order becomes a market order and is executed at 40. The trader thereby holds his loss to 5 points plus commission.

Stop orders can be dangerous in a fast-moving market because prices can run past the trigger quotation. Under the pressure of sudden price declines, the specialist may sell below the stop price at whatever price he can get. At times, when bad news kicks off a chain of stop loss orders in a particular issue, exchange officials may suspend the execution of such orders to enable the specialist to maintain an orderly market.

Odd-Lot Stop Orders

If you are an odd-lot investor—one who buys or sells stocks in less than the 100-share round lot— your order is not executed in the auction market. As explained previously, the odd-lot order is filled by an odd-lot dealer who buys and sells for his own account. The price he pays or receives, however, is tied directly to prices in the round-lot auction market plus the so-called odd-lot differential. The differential on the NYSE is $\frac{1}{8}$ point or $12\frac{1}{2}$ cents a share for stocks selling below $55 a share. At $55 or above, the differential is $\frac{1}{4}$ point or 25 cents a share. For example, if Mrs. Baxter had decided to buy 50 shares of AT&T instead of 100, her broker would have placed the order with the odd-lot dealer. The dealer, who maintains an inventory of AT&T stock, fills the order at a price based on the next 100 share transaction in AT&T, plus either a quarter-point (25 cents) or an eighth ($12\frac{1}{2}$ cents). Thus, Mrs. Baxter would have paid 49¼ for her 50 shares while 100 share lots were selling for 49⅛.

An odd-lot stop order to buy becomes a market order when a round-lot transaction takes place at or above the stop price. An odd-lot stop order to sell becomes a market order when a round-lot transaction takes place at or below the stop price. The market order is then filled at the price of the next round-lot transaction plus the differential in the case of buy orders and minus the differential in the case of sell orders.

Suppose Mr. Jones enters an order to sell 15 shares of AT&T at 50 stop. His order goes directly to an odd-lot broker who is stationed at the AT&T trading post at the New York Exchange. He watches sales take place in the round-lot market at 50½, 50⅜, 50, then 49⅞. He fills the order at 49¾. Mr. Jones's stop order became a market order when the stock sold at 50 and was executed at the price of the next sale, 49⅞, minus the ⅛ point differential.

The stop limit order, in which a limit price is specified as well as a stop price, may also be used by the odd-lot investor. These orders become limited orders when a round-lot transaction takes place at or through the stop price.

Commission Structure   In general, according to the New York Stock Exchange, commissions on the purchase and sale of stock average about 2 percent of the value of·the transaction.

Due to the structure of the commission system, it is advantageous to trade in round lots instead of odd lots and in higher priced shares instead of lower priced stocks. For example, twenty shares of a stock selling for $20—a $400 investment—would cost Mrs. Baxter a buying commission of $12.40, or 3.1 percent of the $400. Furthermore, she would have to pay another commission when she sold the shares. On a purchase of forty shares of the same stock—an investment of $800—the broker's commission would be $20.40, or a little more than 2.5 percent of the $800 investment.

On May 1, 1975, under an SEC order, all fixed commissions on sales on the New York Stock Exchange and other organized exchanges were abolished. The last published commission schedule of the Big Board looked like this from 1972 to 1975:

Single Round Lot Orders

Money Involved In the Order		Minimum Commission
$100 −	$799	2.0% + $ 6.40
800 −	2,499	1.3 + 12.00
2,500 −	19,999	0.9 + 22.00
20,000 −	29,999	0.6 + 82.00
30,000 −	500,000	0.4 + 142.00

(Minimum commission not to exceed $65)

Multiple Round Lot Orders

Money Involved In the Order		Minimum Commission
$100 −	$2,499	1.3% + $12.00
2,500 −	19,999	0.9 + 22.00
20,000 −	29,999	0.6 + 82.00
30,000 −	300,000	0.4 + 142.00

Plus

First to tenth round lot: $6.00 per round lot
Eleventh round lot and more: $4.00 per round lot

The commission on odd-lot orders is figured by using the single round lot rate and subtracting

$2.00. As is the case with single round lot orders, the minimum commission on an odd-lot order is not to exceed $65.

Stockbrokers quickly dubbed May 1, 1975, when fixed commissions ended, "Mayday!" ("M'aider!" being the international distress call of airplane pilots). Actually, no one was hurt.

Some houses announced increases from the previous commission schedule, ranging from 3 to 8 percent—no more than a cent or so per share. This was more than offset for in-and-out traders by extension to stock trading of the thirty-day turn, long a fixture in commodity markets. If a stock is bought and sold, or sold and bought, within thirty days, a single commission is charged. Some houses began to split research and order-taking, offering their informative activities as a separate service. The big institutions continued to negotiate commissions, as they had done for several years.

CHAPTER 9

Marketplace: Over- the- Counter

Although there are about 3,500 stocks listed on the major exchanges, an even wider securities field exists. More than 50,000 stocks are bought and sold each year in the over-the-counter (OTC) market. About 9,500 issues are quoted regularly by OTC dealer-brokers. Perhaps 2,000 of the more active issues are quoted daily or weekly in the financial pages of large daily newspapers.

Since the massive OTC market encompasses all securities not traded on the major exchanges, the quality of its wares varies greatly. It offers opportunities to invest in stocks ranging from high grade issues to the so-called $2 "cats and dogs." The shares of most major banks and insurance companies are traded over-the-counter along with

industrial and merchandising companies, some of
which are the largest in their industries: for
example, American Express Company, Anheuser-
Busch, Baskin-Robbin, Brinks, Inc., and Simon &
Schuster.

Many companies traded on the OTC market
meet or exceed the NYSE standards, which require a listed company to show $16 million in
tangible assets. At the other end of the scale, companies with hardly any assets at all regularly go
public on the OTC market.

Another important difference between listed
and unlisted securities concerns the number of
stockholders. NYSE listing requirements call for
at least 2,000 stockholders, while the AMEX listing requires 750 shareholders with 200,000 shares
outstanding. Consequently, a buyer is almost certain to find a willing seller at some price among
the shareholders of an NYSE or AMEX listed
company. By contrast, the shares of OTC companies usually are held by relatively smaller
numbers of stockholders. Thus, trading can affect
the prices of OTC stocks more sharply than it
affects the prices of securities that are more
widely held.

Why should an investor consider placing a
portion of his funds in over-the-counter securities? *The Over the Counter Securities Handbook,*
which publishes annual descriptions and statistical
data on 2,000 industrial, utility, and financial corporations, suggests these five reasons:

> 1. Many OTC companies are still in the
> early stages of their growth, thus offering
> more possibilities of future long-term capital
> gains than some of the more mature indus-
> trial giants . . . It is worth remembering that

whenever a growing privately-held company needs to raise capital from the public, it *must* come to the over-the-counter market.

2. The OTC market is "home" to many of the so-called "special situations." The special situation is a drastically undervalued, usually little-known issue, which, it is anticipated, will some day spring to spectacular price appreciation.

3. Another factor, often ignored by investors, is the small capitalization of many OTC companies. For example, a company with 10,000 shares outstanding reflects the impact of increased earnings on a one share basis to a far greater degree than a company with 1,000,000 shares. A small capitalization also makes a good basis for stock splits and stock dividends when a company exhibits a strong growth pattern.

4. The investor who is looking for income and stability can also find suitable investment vehicles in the OTC market. Virtually all bank and insurance stocks are traded over-the-counter. Many of these have unbroken dividend records dating back from fifty to over a hundred years. In the industrial and utility category, there are over two hundred unlisted companies which have paid dividends for the past twenty-five to one hundred and eight years.

5. A small unlisted company has a greater chance of being acquired by a larger company, usually on favorable terms to the smaller company. Such a possibility does not exist with most large listed companies.

While the OTC market offers many solid investment opportunities, the pitfalls are numerous. In the late 1960s and 1970, many people suffered severe losses by investing in companies that offered pie-in-the-sky promises. Firms such as nursing homes, franchisers, some computer software companies, and over-expanded conglomerates proved to be bad investments. Many investors, hoping to make quick profits, lost heavily.

Since that period certain restrictions have been imposed by the National Association of Securities Dealers (NASD), a non-profit organization established under the Securities and Exchange Act. The NASD supervises OTC practices and has the power to censure, fine, or expel brokers for misconduct.

The OTC and the listed exchanges differ in their methods of conducting transactions. The exchanges are auction markets, while the OTC is a negotiated market. The exchange member bids for stocks on the exchange trading floor. He tries to buy or sell a stock for his customer at the best possible price. For this service, he receives a commission. The OTC dealer, on the other hand, negotiates prices with other dealers and often with the customer as well.

On an exchange, one specialist makes a market in each listed stock; in the OTC market, as many as thirty-five dealers may have a stock to sell. Thus, when an investor places an order for an OTC security, his broker "shops around," seeking to negotiate the best price. To do this, he uses the OTC "pink sheets," which are circulated daily. The pink sheet contains the previous day's stock prices and the names of the dealers who made a market in various securities. If there are five dealers making a market in a security, exchange rules require the broker to get quotes from three of them.

In February, 1971, an automated quotation service was put into operation. It is called NASDAQ—an acronym for National Association of Securities Dealers Automated Quotations—and radiates from a building in Trumbull, Connecticut, which houses a computer and an acre or so of memory units.

The NASDAQ subscriber has on his desk a small television set with a console like a portable typewriter. By punching a key, a registered representative can ask for a quotation on any one of 5,000 major OTC stocks. His TV set will display five offers or five bids, identified by the code symbols of the dealers, and arrayed in order—up for bids and down for offers.

The market maker to whom the representative gives his order must fill it—but only for 100 shares. That is a dealer-to-dealer price; the broker adds on his commission. If the dealer alters his price, he presses a key for access and tells the Trumbull computer his new figure. The computer knows who is authorized to make markets on what stocks; if someone tries to slip in a quotation on an issue for which he has not formally qualified, the computer flashes what its guiding engineers call the "get lost" sign.

NASDAQ's computer can handle 20,000 stocks a day. It began with 2,000 issues—the ones in which members showed most interest— and has added others from time to time. The list of stocks it actually handles has now passed the 5,000 mark. Big Board stocks like General Motors, AT&T, and Exxon are quoted, and more are being added as the SEC takes a stronger stand against the organized exchanges' efforts to curb the so-called third market in listed stocks.

NASDAQ is beginning to furnish OTC indexes similar to the averages for listed stocks compiled by Dow Jones, Standard & Poor's, the New York Times, and the New York Stock Exchange. These indexes include a composite average for all OTC securities in the NASDAQ system and group averages for transportation, insurance, bank, and industrial issues. In addition, NASDAQ furnishes daily information on buying and selling volume, enabling investors to gauge the performance of their OTC shares. According to William R. Turner, director of NASDAQ, the ready availability of information on OTC securities probably will make these stocks more popular with the investing public. Some officials envision the eventual merger of all the listed and unlisted markets into one huge automated marketplace linking the major exchange and NASDAQ computers.

Selecting an OTC Broker   Finding a helpful specialist in OTC stocks is even more difficult than finding a suitable broker among those who deal on the major exchanges. There are many more OTC dealers to choose from, and the names of firms specializing in unlisted stocks are relatively unknown. An OTC dealer should be more than a mere order taker. He should be more of an analyst and thus better equipped to provide sound investment advice.

OTC specialists often are chosen through recommendations in much the same way as doctors, dentists, or lawyers. Most major brokerage houses that deal in listed securities also provide the services of OTC specialists for their customers. Some of the large wire houses recommend portfolios of OTC stock in their research reports, a practice that is likely to increase as the unlisted market gains stature from the use of NASDAQ.

Samuel Braude, a research analyst specializing in unlisted issues, offers this advice on selecting an OTC dealer: Find out if his expertise matches your investment objectives. He notes that no dealer can be all things to all investors. Be sure the house is a member of the NASD. Most OTC dealers will charge the going stock exchange commission rates for all stocks. A few dealers who are not members of an exchange may use a different schedule of fees. It could be more or less than the fixed exchange fees, but it must be explained to the investor before he does business with the house. "Full disclosure" is the operating rule.

In some cases, the dealer may be acting as a principal, not as a broker. This means he owns, or "has a position in," the stock he is selling. He will charge not a commission but a markup. His profit will be the difference between the price he paid for the stock and the amount for which he sells it.

In the case of stocks selling for more than $10 a share, the NASD allows a maximum gross "spread" (the difference between the bid and the asked price) of 5 percent. The confirmation-of-sales slip should indicate which way the stock was handled. Many OTC stocks, but not all by any means, have a wider "spread" than listed stocks. One reason may be that the issue is thin—that is, the shares are not widely held. Another may be that the stock is not actively traded.

Regardless of the rate of commission charge, assuming of course it is reasonable, the important consideration is the quality of the dealer's investment advice.

New
Issues:
Potentials
and
Pitfalls

One of the chief attractions of the over-the-counter market is the possibility of buying tomorrow's blue chip. A potentially rewarding but sometimes perilous method of getting in on the ground floor is to buy the securities of a company that has just gone public—offered its shares to the investing public for the first time.

While the newly floated securities of a sound, previously privately owned company may offer attractive investment opportunities, the new issues field has been marked by wildly speculative excesses and faddism. For example, one year's fad in uranium stocks may quickly give way to wild speculation in electronics, food franchising, or nursing homes. The SEC requires full disclosure of all pertinent facts about a company. These must be filed on a registration statement and published in a prospectus before the firm makes a public offering of new stocks or bonds. However, when the market is booming, some of the new-issue underwritings border on "con jobs," despite *technical* adherence to the 1933 "Truth in Securities Act."

The traditional SEC full disclosure approach to barring fraudulent new issues promotions is not really dependable, according to David Clurman of the New York State Attorney General's Office. In the Cornell Law Review (November, 1970), Clurman reported the findings of a study of 103 companies that went public in the 1968-69 bull market. According to the report, two out of three companies seeking from $300,000 to $13 million diluted the book value of their public shares from an average of 65 percent to as high as 89 percent. In a majority of the new issues examined, the underwriters obtained warrants (options to buy at a later date) *generally at a price of one cent each*. The "give away" stock involved totalled 5 to 25 percent of the original number of shares issued.

The study indicated that many buyers of new issues operate not on the basis of sound investment values, but on the "bigger fool theory," which predicates selling the stock promptly to bigger fools than themselves. The new issues studied rose rapidly in price from 50 percent to as high as 1,000 percent. Members of the general public who bought the stock afterward did not fare as well. Within seven months, most of the new stocks declined to 40 percent of the original issue price.

Clurman noted that the securities of these companies generally rose in price, frequently beyond all rational value, and then returned to earth when the inevitable cooling-off period began. Investments in these companies rarely were made on the basis of their merits. The atmosphere invited risks; thus, it was easy to rig the game. The big winners were underwriters, insiders of the issuing companies, and people with contacts in these groups. The losers were investors who purchased at inflated prices.

Another pitfall of the OTC market involves stocks issued by a strictly local company, especially one that is family dominated. Such a firm may choose not to pay dividends for years because the family is on the payroll, and their dividends would go largely for income taxes.

Mr. Braude makes these suggestions on new issues:
- Never buy a company that is losing money.
- Stay away from companies that do not show

over-the-counter trading room. These OTC brokers deal in stocks that are not listed on any exchange.

operating sales and earnings for at least the past
three years. This will keep you out of shell corporations that have no actual business operations
or present earnings.

• Stay away from companies that do not show
increasing sales and earnings for at least the past
two years.

• Accept information only from the prospectus.

A frequent weakness of inexperienced investors
in the OTC market is a tendency to buy issues of
companies whose functions or products they do
not fully understand. Often these companies have
scientific-sounding names incorporating such
words as Dynamics, Nuclear, Medical, Electronic,
and so on.

Also, avoid tie-in sales, requiring you to buy
another stock to get an allocation of a "hot issue."
Rumors of pending mergers or expected jumps in
the price of stock can be dangerous when the
stock is a new issue. Sometimes these new issues
do rise sharply, but sometimes the subsequent
plunge is of long duration.

One new issue, a well-known fast-food chain,
was offered at $8 a share early in 1968. It soared
to $30 later that year. By 1971 it was $5 a share
and had sold for even less in the interim.

It is unwise to agree to hold a new issue for a
specified period such as sixty or ninety days.
Once you own a stock, you can sell whenever you
consider the price justifies a sale.

Another important point to investigate is the
proportion of the company's total interest that
has been offered to the public and the price the
public is paying for it compared to the proportion
the management and underwriters get. Sometimes
the management and underwriters reserve for

themselves large blocks of stock, even a controlling interest, at a low price per share; they sell the remainder of the issues to the public at a higher price.

You may demand more qualifications, but those contained in this chapter are the minimums.

CHAPTER 10

Marketplace: Mutual Funds

For the investor of moderate means, who has neither the technical knowledge to invest in stocks outright nor adequate funds to diversify his holdings, investment companies offer both professional management and diversification. These companies pool the funds of many investors to buy stocks, bonds, and other securities. The most widely used is the mutual fund, or open-end investment trust. The investor can buy shares in such a fund at any time and sell them back easily. His sales price will be the current market asset value of the fund's investments. His purchase usually involves a commission, which may be as high as 9 percent.

While mutual funds offer numerous advantages,

they do not eliminate the risks inherent in the stock market. In the long slide through 1973 and 1974 some mutual fund measures showed losses matching those of Standard & Poor's "500," and nearly doubling the fall of the conservative Dow-Jones Industrials.

When mutual fund purchases finally exceeded cash-ins in July, 1974, the reason was the growth of money market short-term funds and tax-exempt bond funds.

Anyone with the foresight to get out of almost any fund early in the slide saved more than enough to offset the commission he would have to pay to get back in after recovery became apparent. The reasoning of holders who were still getting out late in 1974 is harder to fathom; it would seem better to hold for recovery after enduring a two-year bear market, unless one's fund was obviously doing worse than its fellows.

The diversification of mutual funds insures their rise and fall with the market. You cannot select a mutual fund in the belief that they are all similar and will perform in much the same way. There are over 500 mutual funds on the market, and they vary considerably in a number of important respects:

1—*They vary in objective.* Some are more suitable for young people, some for retirees, some for speculators. Others attract conservative investors who are more interested in safeguarding their money at moderate return than in taking risks for big gains.

2—*They vary in performance.* Some have better records of gains in different kinds of markets. Some prove most successful in bull markets.

Others seem better able to withstand bear market declines. In the severe bear market of 1969, for example, some mutual-fund shares lost as much as 40 percent of their value. On the other hand, the average mutual-fund share lost 14.5 percent while the Dow-Jones industrial stock average lost 15.2 percent. Furthermore, a few showed assets on the up side despite the general decline.

3—*Commission fees vary.* The majority of mutual funds are "load type." They charge sales commissions of up to 9.3 percent on investments —more than you would have to pay for direct investment in stocks. A smaller number, known as "no load" funds, charge no sales commission at all.

Which Mutual Fund for You?   How do you choose among the more than 500 mutual funds in operation today? First you must define your investment objectives. Do you want to invest in a fund that strives for high income, or in one that aims for growth of capital?

Do you want to play it safe in a conservative fund that offers a diversified portfolio of blue chip stocks, balanced, perhaps, with some high grade bond holdings? Or would you rather go for broke by investing in the "go-go" funds whose managers invest in small, unseasoned companies and special situations to get quick capital gains or engage in the highly leveraged transactions offered by stock warrants, convertible issues, and buying on margin?

The choices grow even more complex. Hedge funds, which use the techniques of the traditional speculator, buy stocks going up and also try to profit by selling short stocks expected to go down.

Another alternative is the overseas fund—a company that invests in foreign corporations.

Other funds specialize in certain industries such as banks, insurance companies, chemicals, utilities, or oils. Still others, known as new directions funds, invest in companies engaged in scientific and technological research—such fields as birth control, anti-pollution, oceanography, and space-age electronics. The chief appeal of some of the more prominent funds lies in the cult of personality—that is, in the fund manager's reputation for building capital gains.

Closed-End Funds

Mutual funds are classed as open-end investment companies. They issue and sell new shares as long as they can find buyers and stand ready to buy them back. Closed-end investment companies differ from mutual funds. They have a fixed number of shares outstanding and do not trade in their shares. Thus their capitalizations are said to be closed. On occasion, closed-end companies do raise additional funds by sale of additional stock or by public and private offerings of securities.

The shares of many closed-end companies are listed on the New York and other stock exchanges. They are bought and sold like shares of other listed stocks at standard commission rates. Because the shares are traded on the open market, their quoted price reflects how investors appraise the fund as an investment.

In the trough of the 1973-74 bear market, shares of all the closed-end investment companies were selling below asset value, some by 30 percent or more, in anticipation of further market declines.

However, shares of the closed-end funds did not come on the market in volume comparable to the cash-ins of mutual funds. As Malcolm B. Smith, chairman of the Association of Closed-End Investment Companies, pointed out, closed-end funds benefit in hard times because they do not have sales forces to support, and consequently do not feel the mutuals' pressure to perform.

A typical nonsuccess story is that of Advance Investors, which was offered at $15 in April, 1973.

By August, 1974, the fund's assets had dropped to $11.48 a share, and the stock was selling at a further discount of 22 percent or for $8.125 on the NYSE. The asset value rose to $12.08 in April, 1976, but sales by disillusioned shareholders kept the price from rising above $9, which constituted a discount of 26 percent.

In August, 1976, unhappy shareholders forced the conversion of the fund to an open-end company; one-third of the investors then redeemed their shares at asset value. Meanwhile the asset value of the shares continued to decline.

In January, 1977, trustees of the fund were still contending in the annual report that the future belonged to the blue-chip growth stocks, such as Eli Lilly, Perkin-Elmer, and Eastman Kodak, in which the fund concentrates its holdings.

In normal times, the investor should be on the alert for closed-end funds selling below asset values. It may be that the interest of professional investors has simply not caught up with the rising values of the shares in the closed-end fund's portfolio.

Major closed-end investment companies include Adams Express; American European; Carriers & General; Diebold Venture; Dominick Fund; Eurofund; General American Investors; International

Holdings; Japan Fund; Lehman Corporation; Madison Fund; National Aviation; Niagara Corporation; Overseas Securities; Petroleum Corporation; Tri-Continental Corporation; United Corporation; U.S. & Foreign Securities.

Dual Funds

A relatively new development in the mutual fund industry is the dual-purpose investment company, which offers two classes of stock: preferred, or income shares, (usually bought by older investors) and common, or capital shares, (most often purchased by younger investors). Each class of shareholders puts up half the fund's assets and collects either the income or the capital gains achieved by the entire fund. Dual funds operate initially as closed-end investment companies. Eventually (mostly in the early 1980s) they will become open-end funds with their shares redeemable at asset value.

Mutual Fund Services

While all mutual funds offer professional management and portfolio diversification, they also offer a variety of specialized services. These include the following:

1—*Automatic reinvestment.*
This is an option under which all income dividends and capital gains are automatically reinvested in the fund. Through reinvestment, the shareholder maintains and automatically adds to his fund holdings.

2—*Withdrawal plans.*
These enable a shareholder to receive payments

at regular intervals based on the amount he has invested in the fund. Funds usually require a minimum investment to start a withdrawal plan. At times when the market is rising, a fund may be able to make payments out of dividends and capital gains. In a falling market, the shareholder risks reducing his capital to obtain his payments.

3—*Tax-sheltered investment plans.*

The Keogh Act whereby a self-employed person may save on taxes while he builds a retirement fund has been broadened. A self-employed person may now set aside 15 percent of his income, up to $7,500 a year, in such a plan, and deduct the amount from his federal income tax.

If the self-employed investor is an employer, he must contribute a like percentage of the salary of any full-time employee of three years' service to the employee's retirement fund. This is deductible as a business expense.

The Keogh Act now also allows an employee of a firm without a pension plan to contribute, tax exempt, 15 percent of his earnings or $1,500, whichever is less, to an individual retirement account.

Accumulation Plans: Read the Fine Print

When an investor buys shares in most mutual funds, he can choose to participate in an accumulation plan. There are two basic types of plans: voluntary and contractual. In the voluntary plan, once a minimum has been established, the shareholder can invest any amount of money at any time—usually on a monthly or quarterly basis. The contractual plan calls for the shareholder to invest a specific amount of money on a regular basis over a specified period of time.

Of the more than 500 mutual funds now being offered to the investing public, four out of five are load funds, which charge the small investor a sales commmission. Most charge 8.5 percent, which actually comes to 9.3 percent. For example, if you invest $1,000, you pay $85 in sales load and get $915 in shares at the fund's current net asset value. The $85 thus is 9.3 percent of the $915 you invested. A few load funds sell their shares for sales commissions in the neighborhood of 6 percent.

The sales charges exacted by load funds generally exceed the brokerage fees charged for direct stock purchases.

Mutual funds that exact a penalty if the shareholder withdraws from his periodic investment program before completing the contract are known as "front-end load" funds.

For example, the front-end load contract issued by one large investment firm works as follows: The investor agrees to pay a certain amount each month—let's say $40. Of this $40, $1 a month goes to the custodian while $20 is deducted from each of the first twelve payments "to be paid over" to the plan company. Thus only $19 of the investor's $40 monthly payment actually will be credited to his account during each of the first twelve months. At the end of the year his investment will total $480. However, only $228 will actually be invested in the mutual fund; the other $252 will have been used to pay the salesman's commission and the custodial fees.

If an investor in one of these plans finds it hard to continue, he can ask the dealer for a reduction of his monthly investment or for an interruption of payments without penalty. Some contractual plans allow an investor to stop payments for one year. One monthly payment at the end of the year can provide another year's grace if necessary.

In the event of an emergency some dealers will allow the investor to withdraw up to 90 percent without a penalty. If not, he can use the shares as collateral to get a low-cost bank loan.

Even so, the front-end load contract works out inequitably for many buyers. Statistics kept by the mutual funds themselves show that between a fourth and a half of the planholders abandon their plans under circumstances that raise their actual sales load to somewhere between 16 and 20 percent.

However, because the market generally has been rising for the past twenty years, investors who have completed long-term contractual plans have come out ahead.

In December, 1970, after investigations by Congress and the SEC, new regulatory procedures were written into law to lessen the potential for loss in front-end load contracts. The new law provides these alternatives:

1. A fund may continue to charge a 50 percent sales commission for the first year, but if it does so it must agree that the entire transaction can be rescinded within the first forty-five days. Moreover, during the first eighteen months, a shareholder may get a refund of his payments except for a 15 percent commission on the amount he invested.

2. The sales charge may be limited to 20 percent each year for the first three years and 64 percent overall for the first four years.

Most funds offer prospective contractual investors only the 50 percent sales charge option.

Clearly, front-end load contracts are a hazard for the small investor and should be undertaken only if the individual is certain that he will be financially able to complete his investment program.

Contractual plans are prohibited in California, Illinois, Michigan, New Hampshire, Ohio, and Wisconsin. Fund dealers argue that the contractual penalties are beneficial to the small investor since they force him to save. They point out that the front-end load is not unique to mutual funds. Savings-type insurance policies also require policyholders to forfeit part of their payments if they withdraw early.

Periodic investment in mutual funds does make possible dollar averaging at no extra sales cost, since almost all mutual funds permit the reinvestment of dividends and capital gains without an additional sales commission. This useful feature, however, can be achieved by investing in a mutual fund voluntary plan. Under such a plan, you indicate your intention to deposit so much a month, but do not sign a contract. Consequently, you can withdraw without a severe penalty if budgetary problems should arise early in your investment program.

No-Load Funds

About one out of every five funds in the investment company industry is a no-load. This means that stock must be purchased by the investor directly from the fund itself. No-load funds have no salesmen and no sales charge. As a result, the investor saves the 9 percent sales commission, but may pay a higher management fee.

Many no-load funds offer the same services as

load funds. These include dividend reinstatement, withdrawal plans, systematic purchasing, and Keogh plans. Of the more than 140 no-load funds, only a few have redemption charges and, according to the No-Load Mutual Fund Association, this charge is never more than 2 percent.

No-load funds show identical bid and asked prices in the financial columns. Load funds, however, show higher asked prices because of the sales charge. Prospectuses and literature on no-load funds are offered by the home offices of the funds and are often advertised in newspapers. Like load funds, no-loads vary in performance and investment objectives. In general, investment experts agree that carefully selected no-loads deserve serious consideration for the small investor's portfolio.

In some states, savings banks sponsor a mutual fund called the Fund for Mutual Depositors. Shares are sold to depositors of certifying savings banks in the following states at this writing: Alaska, Connecticut, Delaware, Maine, Massachusetts, Minnesota, New Hampshire, New Jersey, New York, Oregon, Pennsylvania, Rhode Island, and Vermont.

Funds of Funds

A recent variation of mutual funds is the "fund of funds." These mutual funds invest only in other mutual funds. By 1972 four were registered with the Securities and Exchange Commission, and others were seeking registration.

Funds of funds relieve the small investor of the burden of choosing one out of more than 500 funds. These funds pay only a small sales load, usually 1½ percent, when they buy shares in other mutual funds because their investments are so large. This compares with the 9 percent that small investors usually pay.

A fund of funds may invest in either load or no-load funds. Some invest in both while at least one, a no-load fund, invests solely in other no-load funds.

Investors in funds of funds pay only a low commission—no more than $1\frac{1}{2}$ percent—to buy shares. Some funds charge no load. That, and the presumably skilled attention the managers give to selecting mutual funds for investment, are the advantages. The disadvantage is that the investor pays two management fees; each is usually $\frac{1}{4}$ to $\frac{1}{2}$ percent of the investment. One goes to the fund of funds; the other, indirectly, to the mutual funds in which his money ultimately is invested.

Advertisements for funds of funds regularly appear in financial magazines and the business pages of newspapers.

Mutual Funds vs. Savings Deposits

How does investing in mutual funds compare with fixed-value forms of saving? Over a long period the average mutual fund does return more than savings accounts or E bonds. Comparisons made by Johnson's Charts, a mutual fund performance charting service widely used by professional investors, showed the following differences in value. At the end of the 1960-69 period, $10,000 left in a savings and loan association had a liquidating value of $10,000 and drew dividends of $4,298. The same amount when left in a savings bank had a liquidating value of $10,000 and dividends of $4,328. The Johnson's Charts mutual

fund average showed a liquidating value of
$14,964 on an investment of $10,000 and dividends
of $1,979. Over the next ten years, however, the
results could be different. And over a short term
you can lose money in mutual funds.

**Funds
vs.
Stocks**
Advisory services that keep track of mutual
fund performance have found that in rising markets the average growth-oriented fund (invested
in stocks rather than partially invested in bonds
or other securities) has risen higher than the stock
market averages. These funds also declined more
than the stock averages in recent bear markets.

The Arthur Lipper Corporation's analysis of
mutual fund performance shows that the average
for 523 mutual funds declined approximately 28
percent in the twelve months from June 30, 1969
to June 30, 1970, compared with declines of 22
percent for the Dow Jones, 26 for the Standard &
Poor's (S & P) 500, and 28 for the American
Stock Exchange index. Then from July 1, 1970 to
June 30, 1971, the Arthur Lipper mutual fund
average went up 40 percent compared to 30 for
the Dow Jones, 37 for the S & P, and 27 for the
AMEX index.

The tendency of some modern mutual funds to
rise and fall more sharply than the stock market
averages indicates that these funds have become
increasingly speculative in comparison to the income and balanced funds which were more representative ten to twenty years ago.

Here is the way mutual funds, listed by objective,
have performed over the last ten years. Lipper
Analytical Services, Inc., of Westfield, New Jersey,
compiled the data. For purposes of comparison,

all dividends and capital gains distributions are assumed to have been reinvested. Figures are percentage changes from original asset value. The longer periods include a disastrous bear market; thus they speak well of mutual funds as a long-term investment.

Objective	10 Years to Dec. 31, 1976	5 Years to Dec. 31, 1976	Year 1976
Capital appreciation funds	+ 23.39	+13.24	+28.51
Growth funds	+ 53.37	−10.71	+18.18
Growth and income funds	+ 90.61	+28.81	+27.54
Balanced funds	+ 73.95	+25.01	+22.11
Income funds	+112.27	+42.47	+25.38

Within these categories, performance varied widely. The most successful growth fund added 475 percent to asset value in ten years; the least successful, .78 of 1 percent. Among income funds in the $100-250 million range, the best performer added 219.50 percent, more than tripling the investor's stake. The least profitable fund registered a 67.79 gain, barely above savings-bank interest.

Selecting Mutual Funds

Important yardsticks for selecting a mutual fund include its performance record, the suitability of its objectives for your investment goals, the sales commission, and the management fee.

Two points deserve special emphasis:

1. As a short-term investment, a load fund charging as much as 8.5 percent sales commission should show very good performance to be worthwhile in comparison to good quality no-load funds.

2. In measuring the potential of various funds, whether load or no-load, compare their records in

resisting downturns as well as their performance
in bull markets. The most suitable fund, especially
if you want to preserve capital as well as increase it, may not be the pace-setter that is on top
in the bull markets, but one that has done well in
the downturns as well as the upswings.

Although a fund's past record is no guarantee
of future success, it is an indication of the management's investment ability. Read the prospectuses of assorted mutual funds. By law these must
state the fund's past record of gains and earnings.

A prospectus charts the progress of an assumed
$10,000 investment over the past ten years (if the
fund has been operating that long). It also shows
the value of the shares each year, the dividends
paid, and the distributions from realized capital
gains.

In addition, the prospectus states the size of the
fund and lists its investments. From this you can
determine whether the fund invests mainly in
blue chips, quality growth stocks, high income
securities, or the non-speculative "businessman's
risks." The prospectus also states the mutual
fund's investment objective. As indicated earlier
in this chapter, funds are usually classified as
"income" funds; "growth" funds; "balanced"
funds, which combine stocks with bonds or preferred shares; and "performance" funds, which
are speculative and volatile.

You can obtain the prospectuses of mutual
funds by writing to their offices. The current performance results of various funds also can be
found in financial services and publications such
as *Wiesenberger's Investment Companies* annual
performance compilation; *Johnson's Charts;*
United's *Mutual Fund Selector;* Lipper Analytical

Services' *Mutual Fund Performance Analysis;* and other financial publications and guides. Some of these financial services are expensive, but they are often available at public libraries.

11

Bonds
and
Preferred
Stocks

The careful investor will seek to balance his port-folio with stable investments that can protect him from downward market fluctuations and generate high current income not provided by growth se-curities. Stable income securities include corporate bonds and preferred stocks.

These securities have long been the preserve of insurance companies, pension funds, and corpo-rate or individual trustees. In fact, not so long ago, savings banks were forbidden to invest in any securities except bonds. Insurance companies are still the largest holders of many types of bonds. They deal in contracts to pay money, without re-gard to the money's value in commodities, and that is what bonds provide.

Trustees of various classes put the funds of widows and orphans into preferred stocks, because the income is usually secure and higher than bond interest. The professional market operator scorned the preferreds as a tails-you-win, heads-I-lose proposition: If a company prospered, its common could go up in proportion, but the preferred's share of earnings was fixed. If the company fell on hard times, the preferred might get nothing for years at a time.

Bonds and preferreds became especially attractive in the early 1970s as their yields rose to 8 to 9 percent. In August, 1971, after the Dow-Jones Industrial Average lost 30 points in a week, United Buying Service, a leading investment adviser, called attention to bond yields on long maturities. The investment service listed eight bonds with Standard & Poor's ratings of A or better, meaning that they would be redeemed at maturity. Each carried a guarantee that it would not be called within five years to be replaced by a bond of lower rate if interest rates fell.

Sixteen months later those bonds sold at an average price of 107, returning a profit of 12 percent. No blue chip stock had paid half as much, and few stocks had equaled this rise.

Unfortunately, as inflation continued unchecked, the bloom on the long-term bond market quickly faded. In August, 1974, United Buying Service's eight best buys were selling for between 69⅝ and 85, an average of perhaps $800 per $1,000 bond. Short-term government notes were yielding 9.9 percent, and a highly regarded utility like Virginia Electric Power was paying 11 percent for long-term money.

That experience reinforces the lesson that bonds

are for long-term money. When the Alabama Power 8½s are redeemed in the year 2001, the buyer, or more likely his child or grandchild, will get back the $1,000 he invested. Meanwhile, the bonds are vulnerable to all the influences that make 5 percent look like a good return one year, and 10 percent appear meager another year.

There is nothing much the investor can do about that fact. Securities of unquestioned worth, like A-rated bonds, all pay about the same return. So if new bonds are selling to yield 10 percent, your older bond will go down to 80, with some possible adjustment for its changing price as redemption date nears.

Bonds are issued in $1,000 denominations. When you see corporate bonds listed in the financial pages, they will be quoted, as for example: "Alabama Power 79." This actually means $790. The listings also describe the bond by its interest rate and its maturity date. In the case of Alabama Power, the interest rate is 8½ percent and maturity is in the year 2001. The interest on bonds and the dividend on preferred stocks are fixed. The $1,000 Alabama Power bond, although it has a market value of $790, will pay 8½ percent of the face value, or $85 a year, until maturity, no matter how much the market price may fluctuate.

How Yields Are Figured   As noted, the market price of a bond may be higher or lower than the original issuing price. With the price of Alabama Power at $790, the investor who bought it at $1,000 would take a loss if he decided to sell. For those who bought it at $790, the yield from the $85 annual interest payment would be 10.8 percent.

To calculate a maturity yield, you simply account for the difference between the 100 percent of principal that the issuer has promised to return to the investor at maturity and the price paid for the bonds. If you pay more than 100 percent, the excess is prorated annually over the life of the bond and subtracted from the yield; if you pay less than 100 percent, the prorated discount is added to the yield.

For instance, suppose a bond that will mature in ten years and pays a 9 percent annual rate of interest on the principal is purchased for 110 percent of the principal amount. The additional 10 percent of principal paid for the bond, if prorated over the 10 years to maturity, would result in a yield reduction of approximately 1 percent a year. Roughly, then, you would earn about 8 percent, instead of 9 percent annually on this bond. If the same bond were bought at 90 percent of the principal, roughly 1 percent per year would be added to the maturity yield to boost the yield from 9 percent to approximately 10 percent.

This rule-of-thumb method, however, fails to take into account the compounding of interest for each year on the difference between the purchase price and the par value. The exact maturity yield may be found in bond tables. To show the difference between a rough and precise computation, the yield on the bond purchased at 110 percent would be 7.53 percent instead of 8 percent, and the bond purchased at 90 percent would yield 10.65 percent instead of 10 percent.

Most bonds are coupon bonds. An 8 percent bond, for example, has a series of $40 interest coupons attached, payable at six-month intervals. Bonds also come in registered form. The paying

agent keeps a record of the owner and sends the
interest payments by check. This is an inconvenience to buyers and sellers, so registered bonds sell
for a point less than coupon bonds of the same
issue.

When bond prices are low and yields are high,
bonds selling for less than their face value often
offer better investment opportunities than new
issues. The interest rate adjusts to the new level,
and there are capital gains if the bonds are held
to maturity. Companies call their outstanding
bonds for redemption when interest rates fall and
it becomes profitable to borrow new money at
lower rates. A bond selling at a discount will not
be called.

Most bonds have provisions that entitle the issuing corporation to pay them off before maturity.
Some bonds, however, offer protection against
redemption to assure investors that they will continue to receive the high interest stated in the
coupon for at least five years. This is an important
point for the investor to remember; otherwise, in
periods of low interest rates, he may be faced with
a reinvestment problem just when it is least advantageous.

A small investor sometimes hesitates to buy
bonds. He may be put off by the long maturity
dates, which range from fifteen to forty years.
Bonds, of course, can be sold before maturity.
There will be a profit or loss, depending on the
state of the market. Bonds which have been issued
for several years have closer maturity dates. Moreover, bonds with relatively short maturities have
been issued during the recent high-interest period
in the hopes that they can be refinanced at a saving at some point several years from now.

In buying bonds, the individual investor, who is mortal, is bidding against the banks or insurance companies, which are not. The institution expects to hold the bond until maturity. For that reason the current yield on a bond differs from the yield to maturity. Yield to maturity takes into account any difference between the price of the bond and its face value. As a result it appears that a short-term bond yields less than a long-term one.

For example, in 1971 a high-quality utility bond, maturing in 1978 and carrying a coupon of $3\frac{3}{4}$ percent, was quoted at 69—a current yield of $5\frac{1}{2}$ percent. However, if the bond were held until maturity, there would be a capital gain of $310, or 45 percent of the $690 investment. The cash inflow of $610—yield plus capital gain—in eight years works out to better than 11 percent.

The same corporation's $4\frac{1}{4}$ percent bonds of 1984 were quoted at 72—a $6\frac{1}{2}$ percent current yield. But again the $280 increase in price, assured to anyone who holds the bond for thirteen years, must be added. The company's 1995 $4\frac{1}{2}$'s were selling for 60 to yield $7\frac{1}{2}$ percent currently. However, the $400 prospective capital gain could be earned only by waiting twenty-four years.

Long-term bonds are more vulnerable to fluctuations in price, because there is time for more ups and downs of interest rates. Even short-term bonds can vary widely, however, and thus should be considered only for long-range savings.

The purchase of bonds, like the purchase of common stocks, requires a careful evaluation of the company. Here are some questions to which a prospective buyer of bonds should find answers:

Judging Bond Quality

- Is the company in an industry that is growing, stagnant, or declining?
- What has been the history of the company's earnings? Were they able to hold up in the worst year to a level that was at least 50 percent of the best year's earnings?
- Is the market value of the company's common stock substantially greater than the total debt represented by its outstanding bonds?

There are many other technical criteria for evaluating bonds. The small investor, like the professional, can be guided by the ratings supplied by Moody's and Standard & Poor's services. Standard & Poor's, for instance, rates the securities in the bond market according to the following formula:

High Grade

AAA—Highest grade, affording the ultimate degree of protection and moving with money rates.

AA—Also high grade, only slightly lower quality, and also moving with general money rates.

Medium or Second Grade

A—Better medium grade with good investment strength. Market behavior will reflect business conditions to some degree.

BBB—Medium grade, susceptible to business conditions, but affording adequate protection.

Speculative

BB—Reasonable investment possibilities, but prone to low earnings and narrow interest coverage in poor periods. Bonds take wide swings as business conditions fluctuate.

B—Speculative. Principal and interest payments are not well assured. The bonds move mainly with the stock market.

CCC and CC—Both outright speculations.

Bonds are traded on the stock exchanges and over-the-counter market through brokers and banks. Because their commission on bonds is less than on stocks, most brokerage houses and bond dealers prefer to sell bond packages of at least $3,000 to $5,000. Bonds are easier to resell in quantity than as single bonds. Until recently, bond commissions were $2.50 per $1,000 bond. Most brokers now charge $5 a bond with a minimum fee of $10.

Odd-lot dealers offer bonds in smaller denominations, the $100 "baby bonds." But when you sell these you must take two points less than the prevailing quotation. Your broker or bank can direct you to odd-lot dealers if they do not handle such transactions themselves.

In recent years, as government anti-inflation policy moved interest rates to all-time highs, investors who bought top-quality corporate bonds were able to nail down an assured future income with a high degree of safety.

Tax Reporting of Bond Interest

It is important to keep a record of the premiums and discounts at which you purchased bonds for use in filing tax returns. The purchase of a bond at a premium means the actual income return from the bond is less than the coupon return. Overlooking this could result in overpayment of the tax. On the other hand, the purchase of a bond at a discount results in the opposite—

the actual income is more than the coupon rate.

How discounts and premiums should be handled for tax purposes varies according to a number of factors, such as type of bond, date issued and date acquired. As noted previously, short-term or intermediate-term bonds bought in the open market for less than face value offer not only the yield, but also a gain taxable at the lower long-term capital gains rate.

Convertibles and Preferreds   The investor goes into bonds seeking certainties: assured yield and the return of his money at a fixed future date. Along with these go two other related certainties: Each year the money he receives as interest will be worth a little less than it was the year before; the bond will be paid off in dollars worth less than the dollars that bought it. Of course, if a bond can be found that will yield 10 percent annually, the investor can accept inflation at a rate of 5 percent a year and still realize savings-bank interest on his money.

However, there are investment instruments that enable an investor to enjoy the security and income offered by bonds and to participate in a company's chances of growth by converting his investment into common stock. Convertible bonds and convertible preferred stocks are issued with an exchange option. They can be converted into a stipulated number of the issuing company's common stock shares. If the common goes up, the convertible securities also will rise; when the common stock declines, the price of the bond is eventually supported by its yield.

There is a price for the convertibility feature, however. Convertible bonds return lower yields

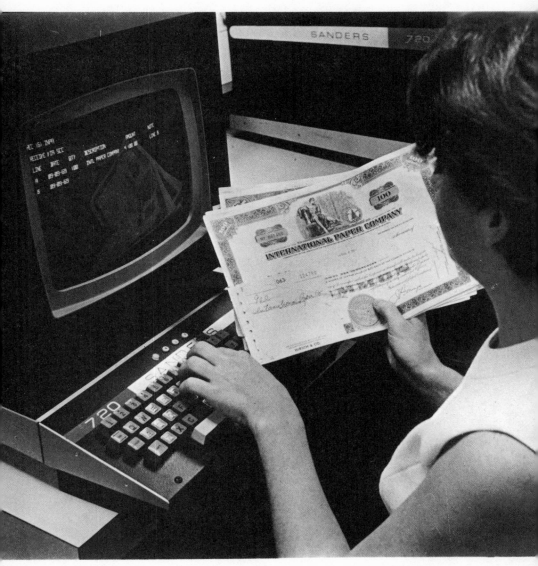

Clerk feeds data on receipt of securities to a computer which displays on television screens an up-to-the-second cash and security position.

than straight bonds, and the investor pays a premium for the conversion privilege. The conversion premium is the difference between the price of the bond and the price of the common stock shares for which it can be exchanged at time of purchase. For example, if a 6 percent convertible bond of XYZ company sold for $980 and carried the right to convert to thirty shares of common stock, the market price of which was $30 (total worth $900), the conversion premium would be $80, or less than 10 percent. This is a moderate price to pay for the option of sharing in future common stock gains.

Conversion premiums range as high as 200 percent, but in general investors consider a premium of more than 25 percent of limited attraction. When the common stock represented by a convertible bond rises substantially above the face value of the bond, companies usually arrange to redeem the bonds. This forces bondholders to convert to common stock.

Good quality convertibles come close to being the ideal investment. They involve small risks and offer good income, the chance to share in potentially large capital gains, and a ready market for resale. The problem, as with all investments, is how to select quality convertibles. It is never advisable to buy a convertible if you would not buy the same company's common stock.

Bond Mutual Funds   Investors lacking the time or technical knowledge to seek out appropriate bond investments may want to investigate the bond and preferred stock mutual funds which specialize in these securities. Some of these open-end funds, whose sales charges are shown in parentheses, are Investors Selective Fund (7.5%) ; Keystone Custodian B-1 (4.4%) ; Keystone Custodian B-2 and B-4 (8.75%) ; National Securities Bond and Preferred Stock Series (8.5%).

There are even closed-end bond funds, although these have not fared well in recent years of soaring interest rates. Some of them are of sufficient size, like American General Bond Fund, to be listed on the Big Board, giving the investor the assurance that he can sell immediately. Dividends of such funds are usually paid monthly.

Extremely high interest rates in the last few years and the accompanying drastic declines in stock prices have turned investors' attention to two new forms of mutual funds—the money market funds, so-called, and the unit investment trust—to such an extent that they deserve a chapter of their own (Chapter 17).

12
Tax-Exempt Bonds

Every year, at income-tax time, we read newspaper accounts of millionaires who have paid no federal income tax. Usually the articles go on to say that the millionaire's fortune is invested in tax-exempt bonds. These bonds are the obligations of states, cities, school districts, and improvement authorities—any state or local governmental unit with taxing power. The language of the bond market groups them all as "municipals."

For people who are gradually moving into higher income-tax brackets, the tax-exemption differential can be of increasing importance. This is especially true since two major factors have raised the coupons on municipals to record levels: interest on all bonds has moved steeply upward;

cities and states are competing strongly for funds
to upgrade schools, roads, and sewage plants.

When a minor executive earned $100 a week in
the forties, the advantage of tax-exemption on a
municipal bond paying 2½ percent, compared
with an industrial bond paying 4 percent, was
trifling. Today the holder of a comparable job
may pay 30 percent in combined state and federal
income taxes. Thus a municipal bond with a 6
percent coupon yields more for him than a corporate bond paying 8½ percent.

Municipal bonds have an advantage over government bonds as well. Government securities
escape the small state income tax, but the municipals escape both state and federal levies. There
is one practical exception to this rule: E bonds,
the popular, small denomination, discount bonds,
although not truly tax-exempt, can be maneuvered
to defer tax liability for almost a lifetime. .

Since the E bond is a discount security, the interest is not taxed until the bond matures and is
cashed in. It is a simple matter to defer one's tax
liability by timing the purchase or by letting the
bond remain in the box after its formal maturity
date. Consequently tax liability arises after retirement. For most of us, lower retirement income, the double exemption for over-65s, and
credits against pension income will have elimi-
nated income taxes from our worries. If still
further tax deferment is desirable, the E bonds
can be exchanged at their matured value for H
bonds, with no taxes payable until the H bonds
mature or are cashed in.*

---

*E bonds have other advantages as a money-managing tool, especially
since their interest rate has moved up to parity with savings bank
interest. They can be purchased in small denominations for a steady
flow of cash after retirement. Redeeming the last purchases first saves
a little on taxes, because the yield rises as maturity approaches.

The Yields You Need on Taxable Securities to Equal Income From Non-Taxable Bonds

TAXABLE INCOME*			TAX-EXEMPT INCOME			
Joint Return	Single Return	Income Tax Bracket	5% tax-free rate equals these taxable yields	5.5% tax-free rate equals these taxable yields	6% tax-free rate equals these taxable yields	6.5% tax-free rate equals these taxable yields
(Thousands)	(Thousands)	(Percent)	(Percent)	(Percent)	(Percent)	(Percent)
	$ 4- 6	21%	6.33%	6.96%	7.59%	8.23%
$ 8- 12		22	6.41	7.05	7.69	8.33
	6- 8	24	6.58	7.24	7.89	8.55
12- 16	8-10	25	6.67	7.33	8.00	8.67
	10-12	27	6.85	7.53	8.22	8.90
16- 20		28	6.94	7.64	8.33	9.03
	12-14	29	7.04	7.75	8.45	9.15
	14-16	31	7.25	7.97	8.70	9.42
20- 24		32	7.35	8.09	8.82	9.56
	16-18	34	7.58	8.33	9.09	9.85
24- 28	18-20	36	7.81	8.59	9.38	10.16
	20-22	38	8.06	8.87	9.68	10.48
28- 32		39	8.20	9.02	9.84	10.66
	22-26	40	8.33	9.17	10.00	10.83
32- 36		42	8.62	9.48	10.34	11.21
36- 40	26-32	45	9.09	10.00	10.91	11.82
40- 44		48	9.62	10.58	11.54	12.50
44- 52	32-38	50	10.00	11.00	12.00	13.00
52- 64		53	10.64	11.70	12.77	13.83
64- 76	38-44	55	11.11	12.22	13.33	14.44
76- 88		58	11.90	13.10	14.29	15.48
88-100	44-50	60	12.50	13.75	15.00	16.25

* Net amount subject to Federal income tax after deductions and exemptions.
Source: Economic Unit, U.S.News & World Report

The higher one's income, of course, the greater the interest-rate advantage of buying municipals. For example, if the individual's top dollar is taxed 50 percent, the yield on a tax-free investment at 5½ percent equals that on a taxed investment at 11 percent.

Municipal bonds fluctuate in value; savings accounts and E bonds do not. However, purchases of municipal bonds can be managed so as to reduce inconvenience from fluctuations. One method of limiting the impact of price fluctuations is to choose several issues with various maturity dates. Thus, short maturities, which provide price stability, can be combined with long maturities, which offer maximum yield. In general, the farther away the due date, the higher the yield; the closer the due date, the less the price fluctuates. **Minimizing Risk**

Municipal bonds usually are recommended for long-term investments, but they also can be selected to yield cash when it will be needed. For example, if you will need cash in seven or eight years to finance your child's education, you could select an issue that will come due at that time.

Two components of return are recognized by the bond dealer: he quotes a bond's "current yield" and its "yield to maturity." Current yield is the percentage found by dividing the price paid for the bond by the amount of its coupon. Yield to maturity is current yield plus a fraction of the difference between the purchase price and the face value. An equal part of that difference is assigned **How to Figure Yield** to each year until the bond is finally redeemed.

While municipal bonds in general have low default risk, the danger of not recovering your full investment is greatest if you buy bonds when interest rates in general are low, and tax-exempt bonds are selling near face value or at a premium above. If interest rates in general rise, the market value of tax-exempts will fall. In that case, if you had to sell the bonds well before their maturity date, you might get back less than you paid.

Tax-exempt bonds are rated by investment services such as Standard & Poor's and Moody's. Lower-rated bonds yield more because of the greater risk of an interruption in payments. An AA bond may yield 5 percent; and a BB bond, 6 percent. Managers of large bond portfolios contend that the differential paid for higher-grade issues is too large; many are skilled at seeking out bonds that are safer than the ratings indicate. In general, it is better to leave such exercises to the pros.

The coupon interest rate listed for a bond in newspaper financial pages is never the actual yield unless the bond is selling exactly at par. For example, "Memphis Electric Revenue 3s 78" at an "asked" price of "84½" means that $1,000 of face-value bonds maturing in 1978 with a coupon of 3 percent (a yield of $30 per $1,000 of original face value) would cost $845 at the current market price. The actual yield to maturity would be 5¾ percent.

Where to Buy Bonds   Tax-exempt bonds can be bought through any stockbroker; the broker will get them from an odd-lot bond dealer. Any commercial bank will buy bonds for a depositor. Commissions are small —perhaps $5 a bond. The broker may waive his commission for a regular customer and settle for a small discount from the bond's seller.

Most municipal bonds issued since 1960 are $5,000 denominations. Earlier bonds were often issued in $1,000 denominations. Small investors, who prefer to invest only $2,000 or so at a time, may have to wait until the bond house has a suitable bond.

It is possible to subscribe directly for a new bond issue. However, some bond underwriters deal only with large institutions. Two of the larger dealers who handle transactions directly with the public as well as with brokers are Lebenthal & Co., One State Street Plaza, New York, New York 10004, and Gibraltar Securities Co., 10 Commerce Court, Newark, New Jersey 07102, and 9100 Wilshire Boulevard, Beverly Hills, California 90212.

Usually there is a spread of about $20 per $1,000 between the bid and asked prices of municipal bonds sold by specialist bond dealers. In effect, this means that a small investor pays the bond dealer a fee or commission of $20 per $1,000 when he buys or sells, or $40 on the round trip. Because of this extra charge, small purchases of bonds are not suitable for short-term investments of two to three years.

You need not report tax-exempt income from local government bonds on your tax return. You do have to pay capital gains tax on any increase in value when you sell or turn in tax-free municipals at maturity. For example, if you pay $4,000 for bonds and receive $5,000 when they become due, you would pay tax on 50 percent of the

$1,000 gain, assuming you held the bonds for at least nine months.

The Revenue Code does not recognize a capital loss when a tax-exempt bond for which a premium has been paid is redeemed at maturity. For example, in November, 1971, a $1,000 bond of New York State, the 6.6 percent issue of 2011, would have cost $1,080. The holder cannot deduct the $80 on his tax return for 2011, as he could if it were a corporation bond.

He can, however, get back his $80 as an expense, called "amortization of bond premium," deducted year by year. In the example given, that would be $2 each year for 40 years. If the bond were sold during any year between purchase and maturity, the seller's cost would be the original $1,080 minus whatever deductions he had taken up to the time of sale.

One question raised in recent years has been the possibility of eliminating the tax exemption on municipal bond interest. Despite much noise about the issue, the possibility does not really exist. The exemption is rooted in Supreme Court decisions dating back to 1819 and was obliquely reaffirmed as recently as January, 1946.

At that time the Court voted, 6 to 2, that New York State must pay a wartime federal sales tax on bottled water from Saratoga Springs, solely because selling spring water was not a governmental activity. Justice William O. Douglas, who only recently retired from the Court, joined the late Justice Hugo L. Black in declaring that the federal government had no right to tax any activity in which a state chose to indulge.

Hence, a Constitutional amendment would be

necessary to end the exemption, and no such amendment is in sight. The states feel that local governments could not possibly finance their growing needs without the exemption. Furthermore, Congress upheld the exemption on municipal bonds in the 1969 Tax Reform Bill.

Tax-Exempt Bond Funds

The development in recent years of mutual funds devoted to tax-exempt bonds enables investors to invest relatively small amounts in tax-exempts. These professionally-managed funds are skilled at selecting high-yielding, but highly-rated bonds, and are better able to diversify than an individual investor. However, their shares involve a sales fee or "load."

For example, the Nuveen Tax-Exempt Bond Fund's sales load is 4½ percent on primary offerings and 5½ on secondary offerings. If the fund yields 6 percent on its portfolio, the sales load would reduce the yield to about 5.7 percent.

Primary offerings of shares in tax-exempt bond funds usually require a minimum investment of $5,000 for fifty $100 units. However, an investor can buy as few as ten units in secondary offerings.

One advantage of tax-exempt bond funds is that the individual investor can redeem his own shares at any time although many of the bonds held by the fund are longer maturities with higher yields. There is no fee or commission for redemptions, but the price of the shares will be at current net asset value. This may be more or less than you originally paid for your shares.

The income yield from shares in a tax-exempt fund also may change from time to time as the fund managers exchange or sell bonds. Proceeds from matured or "called" bonds are distributed to shareholders as a return of principal. They can also be capital gains if portfolio bonds are redeemed or sold at a price above the shareholder's tax cost (the acquisition cost minus any payments received as returns of principal).

In most cases, the interest income from tax-exempt funds is distributed to shareholders every six months. The investor is not required to clip and redeem coupons. However, a tax-exempt bond fund cannot reinvest dividends automatically in contrast to mutual funds, which invest in common stocks and corporate bonds.

The appeal of tax-exempt bonds, however, is subject to changing circumstance. The default of New York City on its short-term paper, along with the widely publicized continuing difficulties facing both the state of New York and New York City, have made the obligations of all cities and states less attractive.

To get the money they need, municipalities of even the highest credit standing have been compelled to pay interest at rates they would not have encountered in more normal times. This narrows the spread between tax-exempt and taxable yields. Consequently, the taxpayer in a lower bracket may be rewarded by taking another look at a class of securities which he may have felt called for surrendering more in yield than could be gained in exemption.

Furthermore, the federal government and the states are now competing to give other favors to lower-income taxpayers, and advantage can be taken of these—such as New Jersey's new homestead tax rebate for the elderly—by reducing one's nominal income.

Tax-Exempt Bond Fund Underwriters

Listed below are leading underwriters of tax-exempt funds:

Bache & Co.	100 Gold Street New York, N.Y. 10038
Hornblower & Weeks-Hemphill, Noyes	8 Hanover Street New York, N.Y. 10004
E. F. Hutton	One Battery Park Plaza New York, N.Y. 10004
Paine, Webber, Jackson & Curtis	425 Park Avenue New York, N.Y. 10005
Shearson Hayden Stone	767 Fifth Avenue New York, N.Y. 10022

(Most of the above firms have offices in principal cities.)

CHAPTER 13

Government Obligations

Investment in obligations of the federal government and its agencies has long been the province
of large investors, banks, and other institutions.
However, in recent years heavy governmental
borrowings in a period of tight money have raised
the yields on Treasury and other agency instruments close to 10 percent. These higher rates have
captured the attention of small investors. This was
especially true in 1969-70, when purchases of
$1,000 were permitted.

In 1970 savings associations and banks com-
plained that savers were drawing out deposits
to buy government instruments. This led the
Treasury and other federal agencies to raise the
minimum limit from $1,000, permitted on short-

term borrowings such as ninety-day Treasury bills, to $10,000.

A number of federal instruments with maturities of one year or more offer longer-term investments. Also, recently developed mutual funds for government securities provide a way to invest in federal obligations, although at a slightly lower rate of earnings.

In 1971 Congress removed the 4½ percent interest ceiling on long-term government bonds, which had been in effect since 1918. The Treasury then offered two issues; one of ten-year bonds at 7.11 percent, and the other of fifty-one-month notes at 7.06 percent. While the fifty-one-month issue required a minimum purchase of $10,000, the long-term issue could be purchased in amounts as low as $1,000.

The Treasury made the longer-term issue available to individual investors largely because of congressional insistence. In exchange, Congress removed the old 4½ percent ceiling. Still the Treasury did not seem eager to sell bonds to individuals in any quantity that would stimulate withdrawals from banks. It priced the long-term bonds to yield only slightly more interest than the simultaneous fifty-one-month issue.

The 7 percent yield on the bonds was significantly higher, at the time they were issued, than the 5 percent customary interest on savings accounts. However, savings banks now offer four-to-seven-year certificates of deposit with rates as high as 7.9 percent. The Federal Reserve Board takes a dim view of this competition. Penalties are exacted if the depositor finds he needs the money before the certificate would normally be paid off.

Treasury securities include short-term bills,

notes, and bonds. The short-term bills are discounted notes that reach their full value in one year or less. An individual who wishes to invest $10,000 can send a certified or cashier's check for $10,000 to any of the regional Federal Reserve offices, say he will accept the "non-competitive average price," and state the desired maturity. Any Federal Reserve Bank or branch provides forms for such tenders.

The buyer receives his bill by registered mail. When he returns it at maturity, he gets a check for the face value of the bill. The difference between the face value and the amount he paid is what he has earned as interest.

Three- and six-month bills are auctioned off every week; nine- and twelve-month bills are sold monthly, on the last day of each month.

Bills are bearer securities and must be handled like cash. They should be kept in a safe-deposit box to protect against loss and returned for redemption by registered mail. Treasury bonds and notes *can* be registered in your name. A Treasury bond is a security maturing in five years or more. If it matures in a shorter time, it is called a note.

Some older series are sold in denominations of $500 or $1,000. On new issues of notes, the denominations are $1,000, $5,000, and higher. Bonds and notes are issued on a regular quarterly cycle and bear interest payable semi-annually.

Where to Buy Notes and Bonds   Older Treasury notes and bonds can be bought on the open market, while new ones can be purchased through any bank. Financial pages of newspapers carry announcements of future issues. Your bank will inform you of these announcements if you request that it provide this service.

Notes and bonds usually are more practical for moderate investors than are short-term bills. In general the notes and bonds pay higher interest than the short-term borrowing. Again 1974 was an exception. A summer issue of ninety-day bills was sold to yield 9 percent, and it was felt that the Treasury might have had to pay more except for general jitters over the prospect that higher-yielding bank paper might turn sour.

There are two other reasons why notes and bonds are more practical than bills: They are available in registered form, and the transaction costs are spread over a longer period. Because dealers, banks, and brokers have increased their charges for handling these transactions, the buying and selling commission on a short round trip can soak up much of the yield.

For example, if a broker or bank charges $5 per $1,000, or $25 for a $5,000 purchase, buying and selling a government instrument would cost at least $50. There also may be an additional service charge of $15 on each transaction. A total commission of $80 on a one-year investment of $5,000 would reduce a 7 percent yield to 5.4 percent. For a two-year round trip the net yield would be 6.2 percent a year.

Obviously, buying notes or bonds for only a year may not be practical.

Many banks and savings associations pay 6 percent on two- to five-year certificates. Some will even take Treasury notes and bills at current bid prices in exchange for 6 percent savings certificates. This is a transaction worth considering when the current effective yield on government securities drops below 6 percent. Furthermore, there is no brokerage fee for the exchange. A bank may charge less commission but may quote a slightly higher price than it paid for the bonds. You could compare the commissions charged by a bank, a broker, and a bond dealer.

If you buy notes or bonds, there may be an advantage in letting a bank handle the transaction if it will hold the securities for you. In 1971 some large brokerage firms announced that they would no longer hold government securities for customers because a major insurance company had discontinued brokerage firms' insurance against loss or theft of bearer-form government securities. Some brokers still provide for the safekeeping of their customers' bearer-form securities through arrangements with banks that have insurance coverage.

In any case, you will pay a little more than the prices quoted in the newspaper financial tables if you buy an "odd lot"—under $100,000 in the case of Treasury instruments.

Other federal agencies issue bonds, notes, and debentures with relatively high yields—generally higher than direct Treasury obligations. These instruments include Federal Land Bank bonds; Federal Home Loan Bank notes; Federal Intermediate Credit Bank debentures; Export-Import Bank obligations; Bank for Cooperatives debentures; Federal National Mortgage Association (FNMA) issues; federal authorities bonds; and issues of urban renewal agencies.

Most of these agencies also have a minimum-purchase level of $10,000 on new issues. Issues in smaller amounts are available through bond dealers and brokers. The Home Loan Bank minimum at this writing is $10,000; the Bank for Cooperatives, $5,000; FNMA, $10,000 for most of its new issues. Only the farm credit agencies still issue new $1,000 notes or bonds. The securities of the farm credit agencies pay a little higher yield because they do not have quite as good credit as the other government agencies. This is due to certain restrictions on their instruments. Furthermore, they are not as widely traded or as liquid.

At yields of 7 to 8 percent, many federal agency bonds and notes, as well as Treasury instruments, are feasible intermediate investments for investors who can afford to invest several thousand dollars.

You can consult *The Bond Buyer*, a financial publication, for information on future issues of both federal and municipal bonds.

Continued inflation during the early 1970s contributed to mistrust of government securities. This caused interest rates to rise, increased government deficits, and thus fueled more inflation. The Keynesian view that the central bank could set the interest rate wherever it wished persisted, and the currency lost value correspondingly.

If the repeated vows of government frugality and fiscal austerity were ever kept, interest rates would fall. Bonds purchased today would rise in price until the approach of their maturity dates moved them back toward the redemption price. Such a course would probably also have a dampening effect on business and hence on prices of common stocks. That would further widen the advantage of bonds over stocks.

However, just a little austerity has been proving too unpopular to be sustained. As that happens, economic stimulus is sought by injecting printing-press money into the nation's supply. Stocks rise;

so do interest rates; and older bonds sell at discounts.

The shorter the maturity of the obligation purchased, of course, the less the danger of the dollar's value changing while the security is held. A look at interest rates will show that a price is extracted for the assurance that the dollar one gets back is as big as the dollar one lends.

Representative banks that act as primary dealers in government securities include the Bankers Trust Co., New York; Chemical Bank New York Trust Co.; Continental Illinois National Bank and Trust Co. of Chicago; the First National Bank of Chicago; First National City Bank, New York; Harris Trust and Savings Bank, Chicago; Morgan Guaranty Trust Co. of New York; United California Bank, Los Angeles.

Leading non-bank dealers, most of whom have branches in major cities, include: Blyth, Eastman Dillon & Co.; Briggs, Schaedle and Co.; Discount Corporation of New York; the First Boston Corporation; Aubrey G. Lanston & Co.; Merrill Lynch, Pierce, Fenner and Smith; William E. Pollock & Co.; Charles E. Quincey & Co.; D. W. Rich & Co.; Salomon Brothers; and the Second District Securities Company.

The Bond Buyer also has a directory of dealers if you prefer to buy directly. The larger dealers have branches in various cities. Usually your broker or bank will use a dealer for odd-lot purchases. You also can ask a dealer to put you on his list to receive periodic lists of quotes for available bonds, the yields, and the smallest amounts available.

One uncomplicated way to participate in the high yields of government securities is through several mutual funds organized for this purpose.

One is the Mutual Fund for Investing in U.S. Government Securities, 701 William Penn Place, Pittsburgh, Pa. 15230. The distributor is Federal Investors, Inc., 421 Seventh Ave., Pittsburgh, Pa. 15219. Shares also can be bought through brokers. The fund has a "low load" of 1½ percent for holdings up to $10,000; less for larger amounts.

Amalgamated Bank of New York offers "USAVE" participation certificates (yielding 6½ percent in mid-1975, payable at maturity and compounded yearly). Certificates are available in maturities of one year, eighteen months, or three years. The offerings may be terminated and renewed from time to time, and the yield may change according to the supply of government securities. The minimum purchase amount is $500. The bank's address is 11 Union Square, New York, N.Y. 10003.

Income Tax Considerations

Unlike state and municipal bonds, the yield on government obligations such as Treasury bills and notes is *not* exempt from federal income tax. However, it *is* exempt from state and local income taxes. Treasury bills do not bear a stated interest, but the difference between the purchase price and the amount you receive on redemption at maturity is considered ordinary income. This must be included in your federal income tax returns, but not in state or local returns.

State and municipal bonds are exempt from the higher federal income tax, while federal obligations escape only the lower state and local taxes. Thus a 6 percent yield from municipal bonds may produce more actual income than 7 percent from federal bills or notes. For retired people, however, the federal obligations, which provide a little more yield, may have more value.

CHAPTER 14

Investment Leverage

Investment leverage enables a small amount of capital to do the work of a larger amount. It is achieved by professional money managers and knowledgeable traders in many ways, depending on their ingenuity and the ever-changing conditions of the market. Common tools used to obtain leverage are margin trading, warrants, and puts and calls.

Margin Trading

To buy on margin, the investor borrows money from his broker, using the securities he purchases as collateral for the loan. The amount a broker can lend is limited by the Federal Reserve Board and the New York Stock Exchange. The Federal

Reserve Board alters its margin requirement from time to time according to its judgment of the market's needs—whether it should be cooled off or warmed up. The NYSE must accept the Federal Reserve's regulation as a minimum, but it can demand 100 percent cash payments on stocks in which it feels trading is out of control.

Fluctuations in margin requirements do not appear to influence the course of stock prices; if speculators believe that there are profits to be made, they will find the money to get into the market.

Of much more importance to the small stock trader—the big institutions do not trade on margin—is a regulation of the Securities and Exchange Commission concerning the money that goes into margin accounts.

During the long 1969-1970 slide in the market, too often it developed that brokerage houses were pledging margined stocks against their total indebtedness. Under these circumstances, a customer's holdings could be endangered if adversity struck the broker and impaired his capital. Therefore, starting December 1, 1972, it became illegal for a broker to use his authorization to pledge margined stock for any purpose except for completing the purchase price he must pay to the seller of stock bought by his customer.

At this writing, permissible margins are 65 percent for common stock, 50 percent for convertible bonds, 30 percent for ordinary corporate bonds, 5 percent for Treasury bills and municipals. This common Wall Street expression is the reverse of the actual situation. The broker does not lend 65 percent of the value of a stock transaction; he lends 35 percent.

Thus, an investor can buy $5,000 worth of XYZ common and put up only $3,250. The broker borrows the other $1,750—35 percent of the stock's cost—from a bank and uses the customer's stock as collateral.

The broker charges an interest rate based on the prime, or call, rate he must pay the bank. Here is a typical margin rate card circulated by a leading broker in 1971 in accordance with the federal "Truth in Lending" regulations.

Under $10,000. . . 2 percent above the call rate.
Under $30,000. . . 1¼ percent above the call
                  rate.
Under $50,000. . . 1 percent above the call rate.
Over $50,000. . . . ¾ percent above the call
                  rate.

If XYZ stock goes up, the investor's leverage, achieved through buying on margin, will bring him a substantial gain. He could then use the increase in the stock's value to make additional margin purchases without putting up additional funds.

Leverage works two ways, however. Suppose the value of the shares drops from $5,000 to $2,250. The investor's broker would call him for more margin money. The investor's equity, after the broker's $1,750 loan is deducted, would be only $500 and thus less than the minimum 25 percent of the market value required by the New York Stock Exchange. If the investor does not supply the added margin money promptly, the broker will sell him out, returning any remaining proceeds from the sale of the stock.

Some conservative brokers have an even higher

maintenance requirement than the 25 percent required by the stock exchange. They may make a
margin call if a customer's equity in the stock
drops below 30 percent of the market value. In
the example of the original $5,000 purchase, which
was bought with a $1,750 loan, the broker would
call for more money if the market price fell below
$2,500. If it dropped to $2,250, leaving an equity
of only $500, the customer would have to put up
an additional $250 to bring it up to 30 percent of
market value.

An investor can make short sales on margin, but
this can entail an additional expense. He must
pay the dividends on the stock borrowed for the
short sale as they become due. In buying on margin, the investor collects the dividends meanwhile.

Another form of leverage is through bank
loans, using stock as collateral. Bankers must ob-
serve the Federal Reserve Board margin requirements when they lend. Consequently, the investor
cannot get any more from a bank than from a
brokerage firm.

Warrants and Rights   Warrants give their holder the right to buy
shares of a corporation's stock at pre-set prices.
Corporations sometimes offer warrants along with
a new stock issue to sweeten a stock offering, especially during periods of tight money. For example,
in 1970 AT&T offered warrants which permitted
buyers of an issue of debentures to buy shares of
common stock at the then-market price even if the
market price subsequently rose higher.

Since some buyers of the stock issue do not
exercise or hold the warrants they receive, but
instead offer them for sale, warrants are often

quoted on the stock exchanges. As investment instruments, warrants possess high leverage. They are a way to make substantial gains on a small investment of capital. You do not have to invest as much to make the same gain as if you bought the stock itself. Take the case of AT&T. In mid-1971 when telephone shares were selling at $43, the warrants were quoted at about $8.25. At that point the stock, then earning $4 a share, had a price-earnings ratio of 11. If you believed that general interest rates, then near unprecedented highs, would decline, thereby stimulating investor interest in utility stocks, and that AT&T would continue its steady earnings growth, you might figure a reasonable future value of the stock at about 16 times earnings or approximately $65.

Suppose you bought fifty shares at $43—an investment of $2,150. If your estimate of $65 was realized, your gain on the rise of $22 would be $1,100. However, that $2,150 would have bought 260 AT&T warrants. If they rose proportionately, the gain would be $5,720.

The risks of buying warrants instead of stock also are increased. If the stock dropped more than $8 (earlier in 1971 AT&T sold at 42), your warrants would have little or no market value. On the other hand, if you had bought fifty shares of the stock itself, you would have retrieved $1,750. Furthermore, while you waited for recovery of your warrants, you would lose the yield your investment would have earned if you had bought stocks instead; in this case, $130 a year.

However, you can obtain some additional leverage without excessive risk by investing a small part of your funds in warrants; in the example of the AT&T stock, you could buy forty shares of the stock and fifty warrants for the same investment.

Puts and Calls   One of the most versatile methods of obtaining investment leverage is the use of options known as puts and calls. These are sometimes used by conservative investors as a hedge, but more often as risky speculations.

A put is a contract which gives the holder the right to sell 100 shares of a stock to the underwriter of the contract at a specified price within a specified time. Puts are bought by investors who believe a stock will go down.

For example, if you expect XYZ stock to drop sharply within a short time, you could buy a ninety-day put for $250—the premium asked by the option writer. Your judgment is correct. The stock drops 10 points before the ninety days are up. Your put is now worth $10 times 100 shares (puts and calls are always based on round lots) or $1,000. Subtracting the premium of $250 leaves a profit of $750.

If your judgment proves wrong and the stock maintains its price or goes up, you let the put lapse. In this case, you lose only your $250 premium, and this can be reduced by listing it as a tax loss.

A call is the opposite of a put. Used by investors who think a stock will go up, the call entitles the contract holder to buy 100 shares of a certain stock from the option writer at a specified price within a specified period.

For example, you are optimistic about the prospects of XYZ stock over the next nine months. Since it sells at $20 a share, you could buy 100 shares for $2,000 plus commission. Instead you buy a nine-month-plus call for a premium of $300. After nine months your stock advances 15 points, a gain of $1,500 on 100 shares. Minus the $300 premium, this gives you a profit of $1,200; since you have held the option for longer than nine months, this profit is treated as a long-term capital gain. If the stock does not rise as anticipated, your out-of-pocket-cost is $300, less the tax loss deduction claimable at the end of the year. Even on your failures, you get a tax write-off.

Conservative investors often use stock options to protect paper profits. By buying a put at the current price of your stock, for example, you can protect yourself against a price decline.

Put and call contracts usually are sold for thirty, sixty, or ninety days, and for nine months-and-five-days. The latter enables the user to qualify for long-term capital gains benefits.

Stockbroker reads latest news developments. The market tends to reflect both the national and world situation.

CHAPTER 15

Agencies That Protect You

Apart from the Securities and Exchange Commission, which will be examined in the next chapter, the securities industry itself has machinery to protect investors from losses—within limits. As the head of one old and respected Wall Street house once said, "The trader's principal complaint boils down to the fact that he bought something to go up and it went down."

There is nothing the industry can do about that. However, the investor will find that most Wall Street houses of standing will attempt to adjust any misunderstanding between the investor and the customer's man. If such adjustment fails—for example, if the investor thinks his account has been churned excessively, or if he has been sold a security through misrepresentation—there are agencies to which an appeal may be taken.

Exchange Complaint Bureaus   The Complaints Division of the New York Stock Exchange employs nine investigators. They handle, free of charge, complaints from investors on matters pertaining to stocks listed on the Big Board. Each complaint by telephone or letter is assigned to an investigator. He elicits the facts surrounding the complaint and draws on his findings to resolve the problem. If a violation of exchange rules is found during an investigation of a complaint, the case is referred to the Big Board's Conduct Division for action.

At the request of the complainant, or in the event the complaint is complex, the matter may be referred to the Office of the Secretary at the exchange for arbitration at a nominal cost. The exchange can draw on more than 400 persons around the country to hear arbitration cases in twelve major U.S. cities, as well as in New York City.

A similar arbitration system for handling complaints is used by the American Stock Exchange, whose members are required to submit to arbitration. Any customer may initiate the proceedings by bringing the facts in his case to the attention of the AMEX's Inquiry Unit.

The AMEX sends a copy of the customer's claim to the member brokerage house and requests a reply. Most disputes are settled at this point.

If a hearing is needed, an arbitration panel is selected. In cases involving a customer, the panel normally consists of three persons chosen by lot. One of these persons is an exchange member;

the second is in the securities industry, but not an exchange member; the third is from a profession other than the securities business.

The fee for an arbitration hearing ranges from $25 for cases involving less than $500 to $120 for claims over $10,000. A deposit is paid by the person requesting that the case be heard. Ultimately, however, the fee is paid by the party against whom the decision is made.

The hearing is held after the close of a business day at the American Stock Exchange. If the customer is situated outside New York City, the hearing can, on request, be held in a more convenient location.

The hearing is somewhat like a court proceeding, but not quite as formal. Testimony is taken, evidence is presented, and there is opportunity for cross-examination of witnesses. Parties to the arbitration may be represented by lawyers. The decision of the panel is binding, and both parties must agree in advance to accept it as such.

The main advantage of arbitration is its speed. While a court case might take several years, arbitration cases usually are settled within three months.

Complaints involving over-the-counter stocks are handled by the Customer Complaint Department of the National Association of Securities Dealers. The NASD requires the aggrieved customer to write a letter outlining his complaint. After the letter is reviewed, the dealer is notified, and an attempt is made to reach a settlement. If no agreement is reached, the dispute can be submitted for arbitration if both customer and dealer agree.

Addresses of the New York Stock Exchange,

AMEX, and NASD complaint departments are:
    Complaints Division, New York Stock Exchange, 11 Wall Street, New York, N.Y. 10005;
    Inquiry Unit, American Stock Exchange, 86 Trinity Place, New York, N.Y. 10006;
    Customer Complaints, National Association of Securities Dealers, 77 Water Street, New York, N.Y. 10004.

Better Business Bureaus   These bureaus were founded sixty years ago in an effort to promote public confidence in private enterprise by setting up a self-regulating system. They are concerned with honesty in securities transactions as part of an overall campaign against false advertising and dishonest selling practices.

The BBB slogan is "Investigate before you invest." They can supply information on the reputation of securities promoters and can help speed up the payments of dividends and the delivery of stock certificates that are held up by confusion and delays in the back offices of brokers and bank transfer agents.

Since the BBBs are voluntary agencies supported by private industry, they have no actual policing or punitive powers. When self-regulation and persuasion fail, however, they often help gather and prepare evidence for law enforcement agencies.

Accredited Better Business Bureaus are located in the following cities:

Alabama: Birmingham, Huntsville, Mobile

Arkansas: Little Rock

Arizona: Phoenix, Tucson

California: Bakersfield, Fresno, Long Beach, Los Angeles, Oakland, Orange, Sacramento, San Bernardino, San Diego, San Francisco, San Jose, San Mateo, Santa Barbara, Stockton, Vallejo, Van Nuys, Walnut Creek

Colorado: Denver

Connecticut: Bridgeport, Hartford, New Haven, Stamford

Delaware: Wilmington

District of Columbia: Washington

Florida: Miami, West Palm Beach

Georgia: Atlanta, Augusta, Columbus, Savannah

Idaho: Boise

Illinois: Chicago, Peoria

Indiana: Elkhart, Fort Wayne, Gary, Indianapolis, South Bend

Iowa: Des Moines, Sioux City

Kansas: Topeka, Wichita

Kentucky: Lexington, Louisville

Louisiana: Baton Rouge, Lake Charles, New Orleans, Shreveport

Maryland: Baltimore

Massachusetts: Boston, Springfield, Worcester

Michigan: Detroit, Grand Rapids

Minnesota: Minneapolis, St. Paul

Missouri: Kansas City, St. Louis, Springfield

Nebraska: Lincoln, Omaha

Nevada: Las Vegas, Reno

New Mexico: Albuquerque

New Jersey: Haddonfield, Paramus, Trenton

New York: Buffalo, Nassau County (Jericho), New York City, Rochester, Schenectady, Syracuse, Utica, White Plains

North Carolina: Charlotte, Greensboro, Winston-Salem

Ohio: Akron, Canton, Cincinnati, Cleveland, Columbus, Dayton, Toledo

Oklahoma: Oklahoma City, Tulsa

Oregon: Portland

Pennsylvania: Philadelphia, Pittsburgh, Scranton

Rhode Island: Providence

South Carolina: Columbia

Tennessee: Chattanooga, Knoxville, Memphis, Nashville

Texas: Amarillo, Austin, Beaumont, Corpus Christi, Dallas, El Paso, Fort Worth, Houston, Lubbock, Midland, San Antonio, Waco

Utah: Salt Lake City

Virginia: Norfolk, Richmond, Roanoke

Washington: Seattle, Spokane, Tacoma, Yakima

Wisconsin: Milwaukee

The postal fraud statute, which was adopted in 1872, can protect the investor from promoters who use the mails to further fraudulent schemes. It can impose criminal penalties—up to five years imprisonment or a $1,000 fine or both—on persons using the mails or causing the mails to be used for illegal schemes. Stocks, oil and gas leases, and savings and loans are some of the major investment areas in which postal inspectors conduct investigations.

The U.S. Postal Service

In some cases, the postal service and the Securities and Exchange Commission will initiate a joint legal action against a fraudulent securities scheme. In other instances, a promoter found guilty of "using the mails to misrepresent" may lose the right to receive through the mail any checks or money orders that relate to the illegal activity. Anyone can get in touch with the postal

inspector in his area through his local post office
or by writing to the Chief Postal Inspector, U.S.
Postal Service, Washington, D.C. 20260.

The State   State attorney generals have responsibility for
Attorney   prosecuting cases in which actual law violations
General   have taken place.

CHAPTER 16

How the Securities and Exchange Commission Works

Securities by their very nature are different from other types of merchandise. The person who buys a new car, a household appliance, or for that matter, a can of beans can inspect the quality of the product and determine the reasonableness of the price in relation to competing products. This is not so with respect to a share of stock or a bond. An engraved certificate representing an interest in an abandoned mine or a defunct gadget manufacturer can look as impressive as a "blue chip" security whose history includes years of unbroken dividend payments.

If the average investor is to make a choice between the security of little or no value and the one that offers a reasonable prospect of satisfactory return, he must take one of these courses:

1—He must make a personal inspection of the properties and operations of the company that issues the securities. However, for all practical purposes this is usually impossible.

2—He must place almost complete reliance on the oral and written representations and available literature about the company, its prospects, and the terms of its securities.

Revelations about stock-selling practices before the market crash of 1929 led to the enactment of the Securities Act of 1933. Since then the Securities and Exchange Commission has required issuers of new securities to disclose publicly all relevant facts needed for evaluation of the risks and prospects of the issues. The stated aim is to protect investors against misrepresentation or concealment. Some Wall Street cynics contend that the very existence of the SEC implies safety to the stock buyer. Consequently, he is lulled to an extent that leaves him as vulnerable as if there were no SEC.

Be that as it may, the individual is still responsible for his investments. The SEC can satisfy itself that the facts essential to informed analysis have been set forth. It cannot go on to bar the sale of securities which such analysis shows to be of little value. In practice, the protection of law is limited by the understanding the investor brings to his reading of the prospectus, or offering circular, which must be issued when a company offers its securities to the public.

The language of a prospectus, by necessity, is legalistic and technical; it may be difficult for the layman to understand. More important, the investor often does not read the prospectus. When he does read it, he may skip over its warnings if the lure of profit is sufficiently strong.

In the later stages of a bull market, gambling fever is high. Dozens of new issues hit the market —baited for unwary investors. These issues exploit the fads of the day—uranium mines, electronics, franchises, or nursing homes. Most such issues come under the SEC's Regulation A, which is designed to help small businessmen raise capital. Regulation A exempts from full SEC regulation an issue of securities for which the total selling price of all shares is less than $300,000. The paperwork and lawyers' fees for securities sold under Regulation A are minimal. Moreover, Regulation A issues are not scrutinized as closely as issues which call for full SEC registration.

A Regulation A company is not required to give as much information as a company that registers under the normal rules. For example, the "Reg A" company does not have to certify its financial statement. Only two years of financial results are required, compared with the five years of audited results for larger companies.

While the prospectus filed with the SEC dutifully observes the letter of the law, "Reg A" issues are frequently marketed by high-pressure salesmen who have few scruples about the truth of their oral claims. To protect themselves against possible legal action resulting from the exaggerated claims of salesmen, underwriters of such securities rely on the formal disclaimer printed in the offering circular. It warns that:

"No dealer, salesman or other person has been authorized to give any information or to make any representation other than those contained in this offering circular, and if given or made, such information or representation must not be relied upon."

In the 1969 study of new stock issues mentioned earlier, David Clurman uncovered numerous instances of conflict between intraoffice brokerage memoranda and offering literature. The former material no doubt provided ammunition for customer's men.

In one case the prospectus contained a "substantial risk" section and a cover legend emphasizing such risks. On the other hand, the confidential underwriter memo contained a section entitled "Factors Limiting Risks," which was intended to help salesmen minimize the impact of the prospectus's risk section. Moreover, some of the names chosen by companies were misleading. One company with the word "aerosystems" in its title was involved mainly in manufacturing ballpoint pens.

There is no direct federal control over the qualifications of securities salesmen. Standards are left largely in the hands of the stock exchanges and industry groups such as the National Association of Securities Dealers, which regulate and police themselves. The SEC can disqualify a salesman for filing false information with the Commission, conviction of a felony or misdemeanor in securities transactions, and willful violation of the securities laws. But by and large, SEC authority over the stock exchanges and over-the-counter dealers lies mostly in reviewing their self-regulatory procedures.

In 1964 Congress extended the truth-in-securities law to require full disclosure reports by companies traded over-the-counter if their assets exceed $1 million and their shareholders number 500 or more. This affected hundreds of corporations. As is the case with securities traded on the major

exchanges, over-the-counter companies now must
file annual and other periodic reports on their
operations.

Investors can inspect this reported information
both at the offices of the SEC and at the stock
exchanges. Such information is also available in
security manuals and through investment services
such as Standard & Poor's and Moody's. Investors
can obtain photocopies of any of the reported data
from SEC offices (listed later in this chapter) at
nominal cost.

In addition to administering the registration
and full disclosure laws, the SEC also restricts
borrowing by brokers and dealers, prohibits the
manipulation of prices and securities traded on
exchanges, directs the furnishing of specified information in connection with proxy solicitations
and provides for the recapture by issuers of short
swing profits resulting from the purchase and sale
of securities by corporate insiders.

The SEC censured more than a dozen institutions which acted on information given by the
president of the Douglas Aircraft Company (now
part of the McDonnell Douglas Corporation) to
Merrill Lynch's underwriting department. The information disclosed a sharp earnings decline several days before the public was told. The shareholders with advance information were able to sell
their Douglas shares to avoid losses, or else to sell
them short for a profit. An estimated $4.5 million
was involved.

One beneficiary of the advance information di-
rected a $3,000 give-up to the Merrill Lynch sales-
man who relayed the inside information to him.
A give-up is a division of the commission between
the executing broker and another broker desig-

nated by the customer. The practice is now prohibited by the New York Stock Exchange.

The SEC has taken steps to deal with the complaints of small investors who get inferior service
or are discouraged from doing business with some
brokerage firms because their orders are small.
One of the conditions the Commission exacted for
the imposition of higher commission rates on stock
trades (which became effective after President
Nixon's 1971 wage and price freeze) was that brokers would maintain service to small customers.

To help the investor avoid unnecessary losses,
the SEC offers this guide to safer investments:

1—Investigate before you invest.

2—Don't deal with strange securities firms.
Consult your broker, banker, or another experienced person you know and trust.

3—Beware of securities offered over the telephone by strangers.

4—Don't listen to high-pressure sales talk.

5—Beware of promises of spectacular profits.

6—Be sure you understand the risks of loss.

7—Don't buy on tips and rumors. Get all the
facts.

8—Tell the salesman to put all information and
advice in writing and mail it to you. Save it.

9—If you don't understand all the written information, consult someone who does.

10—Give at least as much thought to buying a
security as you would to buying any other property costing as much.

It is important to understand what the SEC is
and is not. Losers in the market often go to the
agency for help in recovering their money. That

is not an SEC function; recovery rights for fraud
must be asserted in the courts.

What the SEC *can* do for a defrauded investor
is to uncover the facts which will help him establish his case when he goes to court. Because of its
limited manpower, the agency seldom begins a
suspension or revocation proceeding against a securities house on the basis of an isolated instance
of misconduct; it relies instead on the industry's
self-policing mechanism. But if a pattern of misconduct is established, the agency will move
against the offending company.

SEC staff members complain that in too many
instances the aggrieved investor drops the matter
entirely when he learns that the SEC will not act
as a collection agency for him. This leaves the
agency powerless to proceed.

"They do not seem to realize," a regional staff
lawyer in New York said of one such case, "that
if each investor who runs into a sharpie would
testify against him, we would eventually get the
sharpies out of the Street to everybody's benefit."

The SEC has regional or branch offices in the
following cities:

Regional Offices

Atlanta,	1371 Peachtree St. N.E.
Georgia	30309
Boston,	150 Causeway St.
Massachusetts	02114
Chicago,	Room 1708
Illinois	219 South Dearborn Street
	60604

Denver,	7224 Federal Bldg.,
Colorado	1961 Stout St.
	80202
Fort Worth,	503 U.S. Courthouse,
Texas	10th & Lamar Sts.
	76102
New York,	26 Federal Plaza
New York	10007
Seattle,	900 Hoge Bldg.
Washington	98104
Washington, D.C.	4015 Wilson Blvd.
	Arlington, Va.
	22203

Branch Offices

Cleveland,	Room 779
Ohio	1240 E. 9th at Lakeside
	44109
Detroit,	230 Federal Bldg.
Michigan	48226
Houston,	2606 Federal Office &
Texas	Courts Bldg.
	515 Rusk Ave.
	77002
Los Angeles,	Room 1403
California	U.S. Courthouse
	312 North Spring St.
	90012

Miami, *Florida*	Room 1504 Federal Office Bldg., 51 S.W. First Ave. 33130
Saint Louis, *Missouri*	Room 916 Federal Bldg. 209 North Broadway 63102
Salt Lake City, *Utah*	Room 6004 Federal Bldg., 125 South State St. 84111

17

Money Market Funds and Unit Trusts

As the nation climbed out of the minidepression of the mid-1970s, money market mutual funds were for a brief period the success story of Wall Street. At that time, the stock market was suffering from two sharp declines, and conventional mutual funds, with nothing to advertise but a series of losses in value, were shrinking as redemptions increased.

For a modest entry fee, money market funds allow the small investor to take a medium-term position in the mercurial market for short-term credit —government, financial, mercantile, and industrial —which is centered in New York. The money market fund buys large short-term certificates of deposit from big banks. It invests in ninety-day Treasury bills and the short-term paper of large manufacturers. It advances money to exporters and importers on bankers' acceptances.

By their nature, investments of this kind mature at daily intervals. The money market fund can promise its investors their money back any day. Some funds make it a practice to put a check in the mail the day a request is received—even a request by telephone.

The advantages of investing in a money market fund in times of high short-term interest rates and widespread foreboding about the financial future are many. A ninety-day certificate of deposit in a major bank may yield 11 percent, but such certificates come in denominations of $100,000 or more. Bankers' acceptances carry similar interest rates, but they are placed by brokers who cannot afford to seek out the small investor. Government bills are so close to cash that they require constant custodial care.

Mutual fund managers and financial advisers who were dubious of money market funds pointed to the extreme volatility of short-term interest rates. The chart on page 205 shows how volatile these rates are. Sure enough, interest rates throughout 1976 slid toward a 7 percent "prime"—the rate banks charge their most valued and trustworthy borrowers. Government bills followed the prime rate downward; rates on CDs had to stay below it.

The largest and most successful money market fund, Dreyfus Liquid Assets, offers an instructive case history. Dreyfus, at its peak, had nearly $1 billion in assets. Its yield was a fraction less than 11 percent. That was in the spring of 1976. A year later, in April, 1977, the fund had shrunk to $759 million and its yield had dropped to 4.59 percent. Investors still in the fund were paying an extravagant premium for a little extra liquidity, compared to those who put money into time deposit savings accounts.

The lesson is the principal one this book hopes to teach: There is no foolproof investment; constant vigilance is the price of investment success.

With economic recovery—particularly if it takes the form of a capital goods boom—and continued high government deficits, the day of the money market fund could well come again. Just now, however, these funds are in eclipse.

Unit Investment Trusts   Another new fund nourished by the unusually high interest rates of the past few years is the unit investment trust, which holds corporate bonds. The bonds of highly rated companies, issued years ago with lower coupons, sell at deep discounts. The underwriter of such a fund assembles a portfolio of these bonds and sells participations in multiples of $1,000. The attraction is the gradual disappearance of the discount as the bond's maturity approaches.

Unit investment trusts are strictly long-term investments, to be used for building an estate or a retirement fund. Immediate yields are less than those of new bonds, generally by 1-1½ percent; on the other hand, the yield-to-maturity (see page 149) more than reverses this disadvantage. The fund must be held for several years, however, to receive this benefit.

Obviously, such a fund knows exactly what its income will be until the bonds mature. Its selling price is based on the daily quotations for the bonds in its portfolio. The load is small, no more than 3½ percent. Management is minimized; it consists of clipping coupons. From time to time bonds are paid

The Volatile Money Market's Yields

Yields in percent

Prime Commercial Paper (90 days)

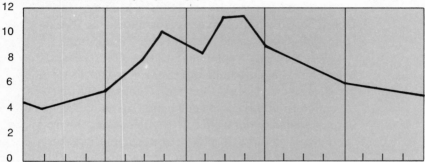

Prime Bankers Acceptances (90 days)

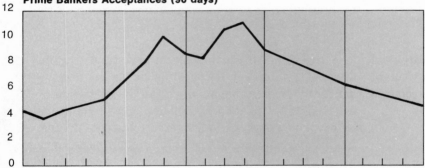

Government Bills (90 days)

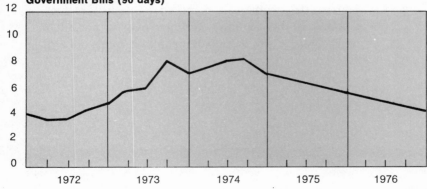

1972 1973 1974 1975 1976

Source: *Federal Reserve Bulletin*

off, creating capital gains and ultimately exhausting the fund. Merrill Lynch; Smith Barney, Harris Upham & Co.; John Nuveen; Hornblower & Weeks-Hemphill, Noyes; and others have these funds.

John Nuveen, a pioneer in the field, recently began a managed bond fund tailored to the needs of investors with Keogh Plan retirement accounts. A managed fund buys and sells bonds instead of keeping a stationary portfolio. At its inception, the first such Nuveen fund proposed to keep the investor's capital gains and income and reinvest them. The investor could draw the whole sum at retirement or bequeath it at death. Since then the fund has been modified to provide some current income.

Individual Retirement Accounts   A new kind of small-scale money fund, the individual retirement account, is being pushed ardently by savings banks since the liberalization of the Keogh Act to allow $1,500 annual contributions by employed persons not covered by pension plans. Each bank calls its plan unique, but in substance what the investor is offered is the transfer of his savings, as soon as they pass $1,000, into the bank's highest-yielding certificate of deposit. The selling point is the ability of compound interest to turn $45,000 in tax-exempt savings, over a period of thirty years, into a $200,000 fund for one's old age.

CHAPTER 18

Taxes
on
Investment
Income

There are a number of special benefits that reduce taxes on investment income. The more you know about these investment tax-savers, the more you may reduce your potential tax liability. That a penny saved is a penny earned is nowhere truer than when reducing taxes on an investment account; a dollar saved is a dollar that goes to work to make more dollars.

Dividend Exclusion

The first $100 of yearly income from certain qualifying dividends on stocks or mutual fund shares is exempt from taxation. This is in recognition of the fact that such income has been taxed once to the corporation that earned it and will be taxed yet again to the shareholder who receives it.

"Dividends" from savings associations or mutual savings banks are interest, not dividends. They get no exclusion. "Dividends" on insurance policies are a return of premiums; they are not income.

If a husband and wife own stocks jointly, they can exclude $200 from their income on a joint return. If the stocks are held in separate names, neither spouse can claim any part of the other's dividends as an exemption. Gifts of shares that will yield $100 a year are often made to dependents who have little or no other income in order to take advantage of the $100 exclusion.

Capital Gains and Losses

If you sell stocks or mutual fund shares at a profit, only one-half of the capital gain is taxable as income if the securities have been held longer than nine months. This extension of the "long-term capital gains" provision of the Revenue Code from six to nine months was enacted in 1976. It is expected that the holding period will be extended to a year beginning in 1978.

If securities are held nine months or less, you pay tax on the total gain. If you wish to sell securities that have risen in value, you should consider whether they qualify as "long-term" investments. The nine-month period begins the day after the day the securities are bought and ends when they are sold.

It is always better to convert dividend income into capital gains, which are taxed about half as much. Here is a method used by professional investors, as reported by Elizabeth Fowler, a financial writer. It involves trading on the tendency of a stock to rise after the company announces a dividend—provided the dividend is a good one.

The method works as follows: After holding a stock for more than nine months, the investor sells it before the ex-dividend date. This is the date on which a new buyer of the shares will not receive the dividend. Under New York Stock Exchange rules, shares usually trade "ex-dividend" beginning four full business days before the date of record.

The date of record is the date on which a company checks its records to determine who owns its stock so that dividend checks can be mailed to the "stockholder of record."

Once the stock sells ex-dividend, the price of the stock customarily goes down. The stockholder of record, who bought the shares before they went ex-dividend, receives the dividend. Meanwhile, the seller of the shares has received the higher price and has converted his dividend income into capital gains. The procedure, of course, assumes that the shareholder is willing to sell his shares.

Net capital loss (excess over gains) can offset up to $1,000 of ordinary taxable income. A loss of more than $1,000 in one year can be carried forward and applied, first against capital gains and then against ordinary income, until the entire loss is "used up." A husband and wife holding securities jointly may use only $1,000 this way, whether they file jointly or separately.

If an individual has more capital losses than gains, he can offset the excess losses against his other income. However, only 50 percent of a long-term capital loss can be used in this way. For example, suppose Mr. Jones has $3,000 of long-term gains and $4,000 of long-term losses. He can reduce his ordinary income by $500 (50 percent of the $1,000 net loss). On the other hand, the full amount of a short-term loss can be deducted from other income to the extent of $1,000 per year.

If an individual has both long- and short-term losses, the rules work as follows: Suppose Mr. Jones has a long-term loss of $600 and a short-term loss of $500. He can offset $800 against his other income—$300 of long-term and the full $500 short-term loss.

Although an excess of short-term losses can be carried forward and offset in full against other income, a carry-forward of long-term losses still is reduced 50 percent. For example, suppose Mr. Jones has a net short-term loss of $500 and a net long-term loss of $2,500. He can subtract the full amount of the net short-term loss from his other income. He can also deduct $500 of the net long-term loss. However, this wipes out $1,000 of the long-term loss. Consequently, he carries forward only $1,500; the offset against future ordinary income will be only 50 percent, or $750. Thus, it usually is advantageous to establish losses before a security is held nine months.

However, an investor also must decide whether it is preferable to wait for a recovery. For example, Mr. Smith buys a stock for $3,000. In a few months its value drops to $2,000. If he sells within the holding period he has a short-term loss of $1,000. In a 28 percent tax bracket, this loss can mean a tax recovery of $280.

When an investor already has long-term losses, it is useful, where possible, to balance these by taking long-term capital gains.

Investors who have losses in securities and wish to take the loss on that year's tax return can maintain their investment position by selling those securities and reinvesting the money in stocks or bonds in the same or a similar industry. Most brokers and bond specialists know how to handle this kind of "tax swap."

An investor who sells securities for less than they cost him cannot claim a loss if he buys the same stock within thirty days before or after the sale. Such a transaction is called a *wash sale*. The loss is simply added to the cost basis for the new shares.

If an investor has bought additional shares of a stock several times during a price decline, he may register a tax loss by selling the first shares he purchases—if the intervals between purchases and sales have been more than the statutory thirty days. For example, Mr. Smith bought 100 shares of a stock at $30 a share, watched it fall to $20, and then bought additional shares to make the average price $25. If he still is not satisfied with the stock's performance, he can sell the original shares before the end of the nine-month holding period and obtain a short-term tax loss. In addition, he may want to keep the more recent lower-priced shares for possible improvement.

If he also owns stocks that have risen in value, Mr. Smith may want to consider the tax advantages of taking short-term losses in one year and long-term gains in another. However, he will have to pay another commission to buy similar new stocks or bonds. This fee must be weighed against the potential tax saving and also against any realistic possibility that his declining stock will recover. On the other hand, the switch might improve his portfolio by substituting a more promising stock.

Sales of corporate bonds to establish losses are

seldom advisable if one intends to reinvest in other bonds because bond prices rarely get out of line with one another. Of course, in a case such as the New Haven, Boston & Maine, and Penn Central bankruptcies, selling out and taking one's losses is the sensible course regardless of tax consequences.

Securities sold on the last business day of the year can establish a tax loss for that year. However, to establish a gain, the investor must sell stocks a few days before the end of the year; the proceeds must be available by the last business day.

Sometimes an investor would like to establish a *gain* for tax purposes before the end of a year, perhaps, because his other income for that year is small, and he expects to make more next year. To establish a gain and still retain the stock, an investor càn sell it and immediately buy it again. There is no thirty-day wash-sale prohibition. However, he should weigh the tax advantage against the additional commission he will pay on these transactions.

If an investor feels a stock has reached its potential, but does not want to pay tax on the gain that year because of substantial other income, he can postpone selling, yet assure a profit, by selling the equivalent shares short or "against the box."

Any gain or loss on a "short" sale is usually treated as a short-term capital gain or loss because the seller actually purchases the stock when he "closes" the transaction. However, under certain circumstances it is possible to have a long-term transaction on a "short" sale. This can occur if the taxpayer owns other shares of the same security and has had them for longer than nine months.

The cost of a stock, in the computation of gains or losses for tax purposes, includes the broker's commission and the federal transfer tax. The proceeds are net proceeds—the amount left after deducting commissions and federal transfer taxes. State transfer taxes on purchases and sales of securities can be deducted from ordinary income if personal deductions are itemized.

Stock dividends frequently pave the way for tax savings. Many corporations pay these dividends in lieu of, or in addition to, cash dividends. Growth companies that prefer to keep all their cash for expansion may pay only stock dividends. In most cases, a stock dividend is not taxable as ordinary income. It merely reduces the investor's cost for each share, in proportion to the number of shares. For example, suppose Mr. Jones owns forty shares that cost $1,000, or $25 a share. A stock dividend of 25 percent increases his stock to fifty shares, with a cost basis of $20 a share. Usually he can count on a greater capital gain when he eventually sells his shares.

Stock and Capital Gains Dividends

Capital gains dividends, which are often paid by mutual funds and other investment companies, are another tax saver. They qualify as capital gains and should not be reported with other dividends, or the investor needlessly will pay full tax rates on them. Usually at the end of the year, the mutual fund or investment company will notify shareholders about dividends that qualify for capital gains treatment or are nontaxable.

Stock rights are papers which give shareholders the right to buy additional stock in a company at a favorable price. They are not taxable as income. If the stockholder sells his rights, he realizes a capital gain—long- or short-term according to the length of time he has owned the stock that entitled him to the rights. If he exercises the rights, he uses the price as the cost basis for his shares.

On stocks acquired by turning in convertible bonds or preferred stock, the holder's cost basis is the amount paid for the original securities. The purchase date, for purposes of determining whether a transaction is long- or short-term, is the previous purchase date of the converted security.

Tax Savings Through Children's Accounts

Some of the tax advantages of shifting investment income to a child or other dependent were reduced by the 1971 changes in the tax laws.

Starting in 1972, any taxpayer for whom another taxpayer could claim a dependency may not shelter any unearned (e.g., investment) income from tax by use of the low-income allowance or the standard deduction. The 15 percent standard deduction and the low-income allowance can be applied only to dependent's *earned* income.

However, since the child still can use his personal exemption against unearned income and since he is in a lower tax bracket to begin with, tax savings can still be realized.

There are two ways to save taxes on money designated for college expenses or other children's needs. One is to give the child cash or stocks to be held under his own name. The other is to give him cash or stocks, but to retain control until a later

date. This can be done through custodian accounts
and trusts.

The simplest method of making outright gifts
is to give the child bonds or cash for his own savings account. Under the "Gifts to Minors" act,
which is valid in all states, an adult can give
securities to a child simply by having them registered in the name of a custodian. The custodian
can be a parent or another family member. For
estate purposes, the custodian should not be the
donor. Otherwise if the donor died, the account
would be taxed as part of his estate.

Under the custodian arrangement, the custodian retains the right to buy and sell shares. He
also can maintain a custodian savings account to
accumulate dividends and other funds which can
be reinvested or left as cash. Cash gifts also can
be deposited in this savings account. You can use
a bank savings account for this purpose in all
states, a savings and loan account in many states,
and credit unions in a few.

While the custodian retains the right to manage the securities and the savings account, the
gift itself is irrevocable. The donor cannot take
back his gifts or use them as collateral for a loan.
He can use the income for funds for the child's
benefit and education, but not to pay for his legal
obligation to support the child. When the child
reaches twenty-one, the donor must turn over to
him the cash and securities in the account.

Brokers, mutual-fund dealers, banks, savings
associations, and credit unions in states which
allow them to be used as depositories for custodian accounts know the procedures for setting
up custodian accounts.

If large amounts such as $15,000 or more are

involved, the individual may decide to set up a trust instead of using the simpler custodian account method. A trust is more flexible as to the age when the child takes over. Furthermore, the donor can give just the income and later get back the principal by creating a short-term trust. It must be in effect at least ten years. Setting up a trust involves legal fees, perhaps $200 for a simple trust, while a custodian account involves no expense at all. A separate trust can be set up for each child, or one trust can be established for several children.

In considering custodian accounts or trusts, note that you can give up to $3,000 a year ($6,000 for a married couple) to each of your children; and you can give a total of $30,000 ($60,000 for a couple) during your lifetime without becoming liable for federal gift tax.

Self-Employed Tax Saver   The limits of the Keogh Act of 1962 on tax-exempt retirement funds for the self-employed have now been raised from $2,500 a year to $7,500 or 15 percent of income, whichever is less, as outlined in Chapter 10. This is much more than a threefold increase actually; the larger sum would be subject to a higher tax. The $7,500 contributor, most often, is giving up $4,500 he could spend and $3,000 that would go to pay federal income tax.

Mutual funds, commercial and savings banks, and stockbrokers are all wooing potential creators of the larger retirement funds. They all have sales points to make. Monte Gordon, vice president of the Dreyfus Corporation, cites these:

• A mutual fund has a host of prototype plans

ready; a tailored plan from a counselor could cost $1,000.

- The mutual fund does the accounting; the investor saves on coping with the red tape of government monitoring.
- Trustee's fees or custodial charges, at the fund's wholesale rate, so to speak, may be as low as 10 percent of a bank's charges.
- The fund keeps up with the law's changes, averting possible unpleasant surprises.

The savings bank makes its appeal on the assured return from its certificates of deposit. As for custodial charges, the savings bank is generally so eager to get the funds that it absorbs those costs.

The stockbroker and his nominee commercial bank allow the retirement-fund builder who wants to try his luck to put his money into the stock market. Capital losses cannot be deducted, but then he does not expect those. Capital gains, which he does expect, are added to the fund untaxed.

Money in a retirement fund cannot be reclaimed for use by the depositor until six months before his sixtieth birthday. Funds are released to his estate if he dies and can be returned to him upon a showing of total or permanent disability. The fund must mature by the time the contributor is six months past the age of seventy.

Just as was the case with the previous smaller retirement funds, the contributor to the larger Keogh Act fund must set aside the same percentage of each permanent employee's earnings as he does of his own. Those are counted as business expenses; a permanent employee is one who has been in an employer's service three years and works at least twenty hours a week.

The individual retirement account for the worker whose employer does not provide a pension is the province of the savings bank. The compound interest is the lure: banks point out how $45,000 deposited over thirty years becomes $200,000. All savings bank plans let deposits accrue in day-to-day accounts until they pass $1,000. Then they are moved into the highest-yielding, longest-term certificate.

Gift and Inheritance Taxes

For years tax reformers fretted over the fact that an heir or gift recipient paid taxes only on capital gains accrued after the gift or bequest came into his possession. The Tax Reform Act of 1976 dealt with this so-called tax avoidance by providing that the tax basis for calculating capital gains should be the price of the securities on December 31, 1976. Losses can only be calculated on the original price of the shares to the donor, not the donee. Here is an example:

Suppose you have a relative who bought Standard Brands common for $9 a share in 1960. He dies and leaves it to you. If you sell it for more than $30.25— the closing price on December 31, 1976—you must pay a gains tax. However, you can only claim a loss if the price falls below $9 a share.

Income Averaging

An individual who has large capital gains in one year along with substantial other income may alleviate the tax effect by using income-averaging. If his income, including taxable capital gains, is at least $3,000 more than 120 percent of his average income in the preceding four years, most of the excess can be spread back over the preceding years and taxed in their top brackets.

An Investment Glossary

Average: A statistical indicator of security price movement. The best known is the Dow-Jones industrial average, which plots price changes of thirty industrial stocks. The average has no meaning with reference to anything but itself. Prices of the stocks in the "Dow" are not divided by thirty to get the average, but by 1.504 to provide continuity after many stock splits and stock dividends. Sales of 1,000 shares in American Can at ¼ down weigh twice as heavily as sales of 10,000 shares of General Motors at a ⅛ point gain.

Bear market: A period of declining prices; the bear's claws point down.

Bearer bond: A bond which does not have the owner's name recorded; its coupons can be clipped and cashed by any holder.

Big board: Universal term for the New York Stock Exchange.

Blue chip: Stock of an investment-grade company of the highest standing; blue chips in poker are worth more than red or white chips..

Bond: The evidence of a corporate, municipal, or government debt, expressed in a stipulated face value, a stipulated rate of interest, and a date at which the issuer will pay the holder the face value of the bond.

Book value: The stated sum of all a company's assets, minus its liabilities, divided by the number of common shares outstanding, is the book value per common share.

Bull market: A period of rising prices; the bull's horns thrust upward.

Capital gain or loss: Profit or loss from the sale of an asset, recognized by the tax laws as differing in kind from profit or loss from the asset's use.

Cash flow: The difference between what a company takes in for sales and services and what it lays out in expenses, taxes, and other costs that must be met immediately. It is a guide to whether current demands can be met, rather than a measure of long-term profitability.

Collateral: Property pledged by a borrower to secure repayment of a loan.

Commission: The broker's fee for buying or selling securities.

Common stock: The shares representing the ownership of a corporation, as distinguished from obligations of various degrees.

Convertible: The term applied to a bond, debenture, or preferred share which may be exchanged by its owner for another security of the issuing company, usually its common stock.

Coupon bond: A bearer bond, so-called because the annual or semi-annual interest payments are made when the coupons attached to the bond are presented to the paying agent.

Cumulative preferred: A preferred stock on which any omitted dividends must be paid before any dividends may be declared on the issuer's common stock.

Dealer: A buyer and seller of securities who maintains an inventory of the issues in which he trades, as distinguished from the broker who acts as the buyer's or seller's agent for a fee.

Debenture: A promissory note secured only by the general credit and assets of a company and usually not backed by a mortgage or lien on any specific assets.

Depletion: An allowance given to companies in the natural resource industries to compensate for the fact that the resources they are exploiting will eventually be used up.

Depreciation: A charge against earnings to compensate for the limited useful lives of plant and machinery. It is calculated to repay the cost of each machine by the time it is worn out.

Dollar averaging: A sytem of buying stocks at regular intervals. A fixed amount regularly invested buys more shares in a low market and fewer in a high market. When averaged over a long term, a relatively low price per share results.

Dow theory: A method of analyzing market trends by observing the movement of the Dow-Jones industrial and transportation averages. A bull market is supposed to continue as long as one average continues to make new highs which are "confirmed" by the other. A reversal is signaled when one average refuses to confirm the other; a bear market is supposed to continue as long as one average makes new lows which are confirmed by the other.

Ex-dividend: Stocks and registered bonds have record dates for the payment of dividends and interest. The New York Stock Exchange sets dates a few days ahead of each one to allow for the physical transfer of the securities. Investors who buy stocks before this day receive this dividend; investors who buy after it do not.

Face value: The amount of the promise to pay. It appears on the face of a fixed-income security.

Fiscal year: A corporation's accounting year. It may not coincide with a calendar year, either by chance or because of some peculiarity of the company's business; e.g., the meat packer's February-through-January year, which ends with the most money in hand and the least meat in storage.

Fixed charges: Expenses such as bond interest, taxes, and royalties, which a company must meet whether it has earnings or not.

Flat: A term referring to securities on which interest and perhaps principal may not be paid. Bonds of bankrupt railroads and income bonds which need not pay when there are no earnings assignable to them are traded flat. Bonds on which interest is being paid are traded "and interest"; the buyer pays the seller the portion of interest assumed to be earned before the sale.

Funded debt: That portion of a corporation's obligations which is expressed in bonds or debentures bearing definite promises to pay fixed interest and to be redeemed at a set date.

General mortgage bond: A bond secured by a blanket mortgage on a corporation's property, often subordinated to specific pledges against certain properties.

Hedging: Protecting oneself against wide market swings by taking both buy and sell positions in a security or commodity.

Income bonds: Bonds which promise to repay principal at a set date, but will pay interest only as it is earned. Often the issuer promises to add any unpaid interest to the face amount of the income bond when it is paid off.

Index: An index differs from an average in that it weighs changes in prices by the size of the companies affected. The Standard & Poor's Index of 400 stocks calculates changes in prices as if all the shares of each company were sold each day, thus giving a giant like General Motors its due influence.

Investment banker: The middleman between the corporation that wants to raise money and the public. When an investment banker or syndicate underwrites a new issue, he or it stands ready to buy the new securities if they cannot be sold to the public.

Investment trust: A company that invests in other companies after which it sells its own shares to the public. If it is a closed-end company, it sells them once and for all. If it is an open-end company, or a mutual fund, it continuously buys and sells its shares.

Leverage: The practice of putting a larger sum at risk than one has in hand by using margin loans, warrants, or puts and calls. These tools multiply one's chances of gain or loss as the market moves. A company is said to be "leveraged" to the degree that it has fixed and limited obligations to holders of securities senior to the common stock. These obligations cause a disproportionate movement up or down in the income available to the common shares.

Liquidity: The degree of ease with which a security can be converted into cash.

Mutual fund: See "Investment trust."

Open order: An order to buy stock, valid until it is executed or countermanded.

Overbought: An opinion that the price of a particular stock, or the prices in the market as a whole, have been pushed to an unstable level by over-eager buying.

Oversold: An opinion that the price of a particular stock or prices in the market as a whole have been pressed to an unstable level by overly pessimistic selling.

Par value: For a stock, the dollar amount assigned each share of stock in the company's charter. For preferred issues and bonds, the value on which the issuer promises to pay dividends.

Participating preferred: A stock entitled to receive a stated dividend before the common stock and part of any dividend thereafter declared on the common stock.

Passed dividend: A dividend not declared at the customary time or at the time the stock market has come to expect one from a company.

Point: For a stock, $1 in price; for a bond, $10 in price.

Preferred stock: A class of stock on which a stated dividend must be paid before the common stock can share in the issuing corporation's earnings.

Premium: A market expression carrying the idea of an excess over an expected norm. A preferred stock or bond selling at a premium brings more than its par value. A new issue that rises quickly from its issuing price sells at a premium. When the redemption price of a bond or preferred issue is higher than par, redemption is at a premium.

Price-earnings ratio: Current market price of a stock divided by twelve-month earnings per share.

Prior preferred: A preferred stock that usually takes precedence over other preferreds issued by the same company.

Profit margin: A measure of earning capacity after taxes; for example, if a company made 20 cents after taxes on each $1 of its sales, its profit margin would be 20 percent.

Prospectus: A circular that describes securities being offered for sale. The prospectus is required by the Securities Act of 1933. Its purpose is full disclosure, especially of any adverse prospects for the issuer.

Proxy: Written authorization permitting someone else to vote a stockholder's shares.

Prudent man rule: In some states, the law provides that a fiduciary, such as a trustee, may invest only in a list of securities designated by the state. In other states, the trustee may invest in a security if a prudent man of discretion and intelligence, who is seeking a reasonable income and preservation of capital, would buy it.

Quotation: This means the highest bid to buy and the lowest offer to sell a security in a given market at a given time. If you ask your broker for a "quote" on a stock, he may say, for example, "26¼ to 26½." This means that $26.25 was the highest price any buyer wanted to pay at the time the quotation was given on the exchange and that $26.50 was the lowest price at which any holder of the stock offered to sell.

Redemption price: The price at which a bond may be repurchased before maturity, or a preferred stock retired, at the option of the issuer.

Registered bond: A bond registered on the books of the issuer's transfer agent. The owner receives the interest by mail rather than by coupon and must endorse the bond to transfer it.

Rights: When a company issues additional stock it often gives its stockholders rights to buy the new shares ahead of other buyers in proportion to the number of shares each owns. In general, the stockholders pay less than the public will be asked to pay.

Secondary distribution: Also known as a secondary offering. This is the resale of a block of stock from a major owner or owners, rather than from the company itself. It is generally sold through an underwriting company or syndicate at a fixed price close to the stock market's valuation of the shares, but without sales commission or odd-lot differential.

Selling against the box: This is a short sale undertaken to protect a profit in a stock and to defer tax liability to another year. For example, an investor owns 100 shares of XYZ which has gone up and which he thinks may decline. Consequently, he sells the 100 shares "short" and keeps them. If XYZ declines, the profit on his short sale is exactly offset by the loss in the market value of the stock he owns. If XYZ advances, the loss on his short sale is offset by the gain in the market value of the stock he has retained.

Serial bond: An issue that matures in small amounts at periodic intervals. Railroad equipment notes and municipal improvement issues are commonly serial bonds.

Short sale: Sale of a stock the seller does not own, in the belief that it can be bought later at a lower price.

Specialist: The stock exchange member who undertakes to keep an orderly market in a specified stock by buying or selling on his own account when bids and offers by the public are not matched well enough to maintain an orderly market. He is the broker's broker in the stock in which he specializes and receives commissions for executing other brokers' orders.

Stock ahead: The explanation given to an investor who, after entering an order to buy or sell stock at a specified price, sees other transactions reported at that price while his is not. The reason: the specialist received other orders at that price ahead of his.

Tax-exempt bond: A bond which pays no federal taxes because it is issued by a state or a subordinate division of a state.

Technical position: The term covering the internal factors affecting the market, as opposed to fundamental forces such as prosperity or recession.

Thin market: The market for a stock is thin when buying or selling a few shares can affect its price disproportionately in either direction.

Transfer agent: The institution that keeps a record of each stockholder, his address, and the number of shares he owns. It sees that certificates are issued and cancelled as stocks change ownership.

Warrant: A paper giving its holder the right to buy a security at a set price, either within a specified period or perpetually. A warrant is generally offered with another security as an added inducement to buy.

Index

diversification *(continued)*
  small investments, 35-36
  solo investing, 32-35
dividend exclusion, 207-208
dividends:
  OTC stock, 119
  rate, 38
  working with broker, 76
dividend yield. *See* yield
dollar averaging:
  diversification, 33-34
  seasonal trends and, 63-64
Dominick Fund, 134
double bottom (market signal), 60
double top (market signal), 60
Douglas Aircraft Company, 197
Douglas, William O., 164
Dow, Charles H., 58-59
Dow-Jones averages, 46, 62, 80,
  122
downturns. *See* bear markets
Dreyfus Corporation, 18, 216
Dreyfus Liquid Assets, 203-204
drug companies, income stocks, 51
dual-purpose investment company,
  135

E
E bonds (Treasury Dept.), 28, 159
earned growth rate, 94
earnings:
  minimum exchange requirements,
    104
  OTC companies, 125-128
  per share, financial report, 92
  rates and trends, 38-44
  retained, 98
ecological problems, 57
economic outlook, building
  portfolios, 30
education:
  facilities, 48
  fixed-value savings for, 28
  taxes on savings for, 214
electric utilities, P/Es, 52
Ellis, Charles D., 87-88
emergencies (personal), mutual
  fund withdrawals, 137-138

emotions, affecting decisions, 32
equities, percentage of income in,
  29
Eurofund, 134
"everybody knows more than
  anybody," 31
exchanges. *See* securities exchanges
executives, president's letter, 100
Export-Import Bank obligations,
  172

F
FNMA. *See* Federal National
  Mortgage Association
faddism:
  OTC stocks, 124
  P/Es and, 45
  SEC and, 195
Fall (season). *See* Autumn Sell-Off
family-dominated companies, OTC
  stock, 125
federal government obligations.
  See government obligations
Federal Home Loan Bank notes,
  172
Federal Intermediate Credit Bank
  debentures, 172
Federal Investors, 175
Federal Land Bank bonds, 172
Federal National Mortgage
  Association issues, 172
fees:
  arbitration hearing, 187
  investment counselors, 83-85
  OTC stock, 123
First Boston Corporation, 174
First National Bank of Chicago,
  174
First National City Bank of New
  York, 75, 174
five-or-ten-year summary, financial
  reports, 98
fixed-value savings, 25-28
floor broker, 105
follow the leader (error), 31
food service, OTC stock, 128
footnotes, financial reports, 99
Fowler, Elizabeth, 208

PHOTO CREDITS

U.S.News & World Report
Warren K. Leffler—71
Thomas J. O'Halloran—126-127; 184
Marion S. Trikosko—12